Old
Country
Cookin'

❧ AMISH COOKING ❧

Brookside Bookstore
420 Weaver Rd.
Millersburg, PA 17061

ISBN 0-9642548-9-1

CARLISLE
PRINTING
♦ Walnut Creek ♦

2727 Twp. Rd. 421 • Sugarcreek, Ohio 44681

Introduction

This book contains over 300 recipes for home baking, cooking and canning. They consist of old hand-me-down recipes which are our favorites. Some newer recipes are also included.

Due to the high costs of living, home baking and canning seem necessary. Gardening is also treasured in the hearts of those who enjoy stirring up a home cooked meal! We hope our recipes will encourage curiosity. . .

❧

Beatitudes for Homemakers

Blessed is she whose daily tasks are a work of love; for her willing hand and happy heart transform duty into joyous service to all her family and God.

Blessed is she who opens the door to welcome stranger and well-loved friends; for gracious hospitality is a test of brotherly love.

Blessed is she who mends both stockings and broken toys and broken hearts; for her understanding is a balm to her husband and children.

Blessed is she who scours and scrubs; for well she knows that cleanliness is one expression of godliness.

Blessed is she whom children love; for the love of a child is of greater value than fortune or fame.

Blessed is she who sings in her work; for music lightens the heaviest load and brightens the dullest chore.

Blessed is she who dusts away doubt and fear and sweeps all the cobwebs of confusion; for her faith will triumph over all adversity.

Blessed is she who serves laughter and smiles with every meal; for her cheerfulness is an aid to mental and physical digestion.

Blessed is she who introduces Jesus Christ to her children; for godly sons and daughters shall be her reward.

Blessed is she who preserves the sacredness of the Christian home; for hers is a divine trust that crowns her with dignity.

Dedication

We dedicate this book to our Mothers and Grandmothers, for teaching us the joy and pleasure of baking and cooking, an art you have taught your daughters while still very young and willing to learn.

⁊ⱥ

"To Our Mothers and Grandmothers"

Your hand has rocked the cradle
   For little ones so dear
You soothed their fretful heartaches,
   You dried their falling tear.

You've been a nurse and teacher,
   A secretary, too
You cooked and washed and mended;
   There was so much to do!

You laid a firm foundation
   Through every passing day
You taught God's word so steadfast,
   And told us how to pray.

You emphasized the virtues
   Of faith and charity,
Of walking close to Jesus
   In deep humility!

The passing years are fleeting
   Gray hairs adorn your brow.
Life's sun is traveling westward,
   Its rays are fainter now!

The pathway worn and weary
   With trials will be past;
And in a home eternal
   There'll be sweet rest, at last!

"The art of making sauerkraut"

SauerKraut
(A quick easy way to make SauerKraut)

Shred the cabbage and pack into jars not very tight. Make a hole down through the middle with a wooden spoon or similar utensil and put in a tablespoon of salt to each quart. Then fill with boiling water and seal your jars tightly, at once. Will be ready to use in 4 to 6 weeks. More salt may be added if desired.

Enjoying a mid-day snack at harvest time many years ago

Sugar Cookies

7 eggs
4 tsp. soda
4 c. brown sugar
1 Tbsp. vinegar

2 c. Wesson oil
1 can Carnation milk
6 c. flour

Pour vinegar on soda and beat with eggs until fluffy. Mix remaining ingredients well.

Topping:
1 c. granulated sugar
1 c. brown sugar

1 tsp. cinnamon

Put topping on cookies before baking. Bake at 350° for approx. 12 min.

The dinner horn — Old-time equivalent for "Come and get it!"

Good Beef Stew

2 lb. beef stew meat, cut into 1" pieces
1/3 c. all-purpose flour
1/4 c. vegetable oil
1/2 c. snipped parsley
3 Tbsp. packed brown sugar
1 Tbsp. salt
1/2 tsp. dried rosemary leaves (if desired)

1 c. (10 1/2 oz.) condensed beef broth
1/4 c. vinegar
1 large onion, sliced
1 small clove garlic, crushed
6 large potatoes
2 carrots (if desired)

Heat oven to 325°. Coat beef pieces with flour. Brown beef, a few pieces at a time, in oil in pan over medium heat; drain. Remove beef from pan. Mix parsley, brown sugar and salt in pan. Stir in broth and vinegar gradually, scraping bottom of pan until gravy is smooth. Heat to boiling, stirring constantly. Stir in onion, garlic and beef. Add potatoes. Cover and bake in casserole until beef and potatoes are tender, about 3 hours. Excellent!

7

Gaarde Sache

Arbeera

Speck

Schneid Bad

Sols un Peffer

Milich

Brot

Our Talk

Our talk ain't so for fanciness,
　　But plain, it makes just right.
It ain't so good dressed up in print,
　　But from the heart it comes out bright.

It gets around to all the things
　　We know and have to say,
It sticks to us like "boowalice,"
　　It's as rich as good red clay.

When people listen once they think
　　We don't know English none,
But at the County Fair you see
　　The prize our Melly won.

You can't redd up the world and make
　　All people talk the same.
The Pennsylvania Deitsch is ourn,
　　And yourn is what you name.

Oier

Buuna

Offe

8

God Has Blessed America

Our country God has richly blessed
   With foods and eats, so many,
So that it might be referred to as,
   "The land of milk and honey."

But did we ever stop to think,
   Not all lands have such wealth?
Some may be quite hungry,
   Not food enough for health.

While for our meals we serve so much
   Rich foods we like to taste,
Then for our health it is not good,
   And perhaps some goes to waste.

Might we not displease our Lord,
   Serving more than for our good?
Or would we show our thankfulness
   By decorating food?

God has given; God could take!
   It's all within His power;
We know not at all what might befall
   Within a coming hour.

Someday, sometime, we might be made
   To think back to our past,
Of all the foods we wasted,
   We then could only gasp!

Yes, God has blessed America,
   So let us try with prayer,
To use the blessings rightfully,
   And with the needy share.

                     ﻬ

Table of Contents

Thumb Index

Each of the 12 different categories in this cook-book are designated with a "thumb finder."

Simply fan the front edge of the book and find the page that corresponds with the solid bar on this page.

Soups

Salads, Sandwiches and Drink

Meats and Vegetables

Cakes

Cookies

Pies

Breads and Rolls

Desserts

Breakfast and Jellies

Preserving Foods

Miscellaneous

Helpful Hints

Apple Butter
(Lotwaerick)

4 qts. apples
2 qts. water
1½ qts. cider
1½ lbs. sugar

1 tsp. cinnamon
1 tsp. allspice
1 tsp. cloves

Wash and slice apples. Cover with water and boil till soft. Press through sieve to remove skins and seeds. Bring cider to boil, add apple pulp and sugar, cook till it thickens, stirring constantly. Add spices, cook till thick enough to spread. Pour in jars and seal.

Rivel Soup

2 c. unsifted flour
½ tsp. salt
1 egg, well beaten

Chicken or beef broth
1 can crushed corn

Combine the flour, salt and beaten egg and mix together with the fingers until mixture is crumbly. Drop this mixture into the broth, add the corn and simmer about 10 min. The rivels will look like boiled rice when cooked. Rivel means lump.

Pigs Stomach Recipe

1 well cleaned pig stomach
1 onion, cut fine
1 green pepper, diced
2 stalks celery, cut fine
3 c. diced potatoes

Minced parsley
Black pepper
1 tsp. salt
Smoked sausage and spare ribs

Mix onion, green pepper, celery, potatoes, parsley, pepper and salt before adding cut smoked sausage and spare ribs (cut into serving pieces).
Stuff pig stomach with above mixture and close with cooking clips. Bake at 350° for 2 hrs.

A Mother's Prayer

I wash the dirt from little feet
   And as I wash I pray
Lord keep them ever pure and true
   To walk the narrow way.

I wash the dirt from little hands
   And earnestly I ask
"Lord may they ever yielded be
   To do the humblest task."

I wash the dirt from little knees,
   And pray Lord, may they be,
The place where victories are won
   And blessings sought from Thee.

I wash the clothes that soil so soon,
   And as I the children dress,
Pray may their clothes through ages be,
   The robe of righteousness.

E're many hours shall pass I know,
   I'll wash these hands again,
And there'll be dirt upon their clothes
   Before the day shall end.

But as they journey on through life
   And learn of want and pain,
Lord, keep their precious little hearts,
   Cleansed from all sin and stain.

For soap and water cannot reach
   Where thou alone canst see,
Their hands and feet, these I can wash,
   I trust their hearts to Thee.

❧

❧ Notes ❧

_____

_____

_____

_____

_____

_____

_____

_____

_____

_____

_____

_____

_____

_____

_____

_____

_____   ❧

Soups

&

Thanksgiving Prayer

Thank You, God, for everything–
The big things and the small,
For "every good gift comes from God,"
The giver of them all,
And all too often we accept
Without any thanks or praise
The gifts God sends as blessing
Each day in many ways,
And so at this Thanksgiving time
We offer up a prayer
To thank You, God, for giving us
A lot more than our share . . .
To thank You for the little things
That often come our way,
The things we take for granted
But don't mention when we pray.
The unexpected courtesy,
The thoughtful, kindly deed,
A hand reached out to help us
In the time of sudden need . . .
Oh, make us more aware, dear God,
Of little daily graces
That come to us with "sweet surprise"
From never-dreamed-of places.
Then, thank You for the "miracles"
We are much too blind to see,
And give us new awareness
Of our many gifts from Thee,
And help us to remember
That the key to life and living
Is to make each prayer a prayer of thanks,
And every day Thanksgiving.

Easy Ham and Bean Soup

3 c. leftover ham
$^1/_4$ c. chopped onion
$^1/_2$ c. chopped celery

2 c. (canned) Great Northern beans
Small amount of parsley

Use ham broth and cook all ingredients for 15 min. Then add 4 Tbsp. browned butter and as much milk as desired. Thicken with a little flour.

Oyster Stew

12 fresh oysters
4 Tbsp. butter

3 pts. milk
1 Tbsp. salt (scant)

Kessel

Fry oysters in butter for 10 min. Add milk and salt and bring to a boil. Serve with crackers.

Rice Chicken Soup

4 lbs. chicken
2 c. diced carrots
2 c. diced celery
1 lb. noodles
$^1/_2$ c. rice

1 c. diced potato
1/2 c. diced onion
1 qt. corn
Salt and pepper to taste

Cook chicken, then debone it and save the broth. Add water to make 1 gal. liquid. Boil potatoes, carrots and celery in broth till tender. Then add noodles, rice, onion and corn and simmer until done.

Let us not forget to be more grateful to the Giver of our food
than to the one who has prepared it. ❧

Vegetable Soup

1 qt. potatoes
1 qt. carrots
1 qt. corn
1 qt. green beans
1 qt. chopped onions
1 pkg. (1 lb.) soup beans
1 qt. celery

1 qt. spaghetti or alphabets, cooked
6 or 7 qt. tomato juice
1/2 c. brown sugar
3 lb. hamburger
1 tsp. chili powder
12 beef cubes
1 box (11 oz.) beef broth powder

Soak beans overnight. Cook celery. Fry hamburg in 1/4 lb. butter or bake in butter at 300° for several hrs. Chop until fine. Cook vegetables in salt, not quite soft, then mix together and cold pack 2 hrs. Makes 15 qt. Don't make jars more than 3/4 full.

Chicken Corn Soup

3 1/2 lb. stewing chicken with bone
3 - 4 c. water
1 1/2 pt. corn
1/2 c. chopped celery
1 1/2 tsp. salt

1 sm. onion, chopped
1/2 c. noodles, broken
2 hard boiled eggs, chopped
1 chicken bouillon cube

Cook chicken and salt in water till tender. Separate chicken from broth and cut in small pieces. Use broth and cook chicken with vegetables and noodles for about 30 min. on low after it comes to a boil. Add eggs and serve very hot. You may need to add more water for broth. For extra flavor you can add bouillon cube to broth while cooking.

Cream of Corn Soup

2 c. water
2 c. canned corn
1/2 c. celery, chopped
1/2 c. parsley, chopped
2 c. milk

1 Tbsp. onion, chopped
2 Tbsp. butter
2 Tbsp. flour
1 tsp. salt
Dash of pepper

Cook all vegetables until tender. Add butter, milk and flour last.

Cheesy Broccoli Soup

1/4 c. chopped onion
1 Tbsp. margarine
1 1/2 c. milk

3/4 lb. Velveeta cheese, cubed
1 (10 oz.) pkg. frozen broccoli
Dash of pepper

In a 2 qt. sauce pan, sauté onion in margarine until tender. Add remaining ingredients; stir over low heat until cheese spread is melted and mixture is hot. Top each serving with toasted slivered almonds, if desired. Makes 4 3/4 c. servings.

Potato Broccoli Soup

1 c. chopped broccoli
4 c. diced potatoes
3 eggs, optional

1/4 c. chicken broth mix or
1 can cream of chicken soup
2 c. milk

Add water to broccoli and potatoes; bring to a boil. Add raw eggs and cook until vegetables are soft. Use potato masher and mash slightly. Add chicken mix and stir. Add milk and heat slowly.

Potato Cream Soup

2 c. raw potatoes, diced
2 stalks celery, diced
2 onions, minced
2 1/2 c. water
3 1/2 Tbsp. flour

1 1/2 tsp. salt
3 tsp. butter
2 c. milk
1/4 tsp. pepper

Cook potatoes, onion and celery in boiling water. Melt butter in double boiler. Add flour, then milk and seasoning. Cook until mixture is thick and smooth. Rub the potato mixture through a sieve. Add the white sauce. Garnish with parsley to serve. Add a few slices of your favorite cheese if you wish.

Potato Soup

2 med. potatoes
1 med. onion
Noodles
1 qt. milk

Salt and pepper to taste
Butter
1/2 c. Velveeta cheese

Peel and cut potatoes in small cubes. Boil potatoes and onion in salt water until about half done. Add noodles and cook until tender. Add the milk and bring to a boil, then add butter and salt to suit taste. Add cheese and stir till melted. Serve with Ritz crackers. Delicious!

Grummbier

Tomato Soup to Can

6 onions
1 bunch celery
8 qt. fresh tomatoes
1 c. sugar

1/4 c. salt
1 c. butter
1 c. flour

Cook tomatoes, onions and chopped celery until tender. Put through strainer. Add sugar and salt. Cream butter and flour and add to juice. Blend well and simmer until slightly thickened. Cook as long as you do for gravy. Put boiling soup in jars and seal. (When serving; add a pinch of baking soda. Heat slightly, stirring in an equal amount of milk.) Makes 12 pints.

Cream of Tomato Soup

1 tsp. chopped onion
2 Tbsp. butter
3 Tbsp. flour
2 tsp. sugar

1 tsp. salt
1/8 tsp. pepper
2 c. tomato juice
2 c. cold milk

Sauté onion in butter; stir in rest of ingredients, except juice and milk. Cook until smooth and bubbly. Gradually stir in juice; bring to a boil. Gradually add milk.

Cream of Celery Soup

2 heads celery
1 qt. water
1 qt. hot milk
2 Tbsp. flour

2 Tbsp. butter
1 Tbsp. minced parsley
1/2 c. cream

Zelerich

Dice celery, using a few leaves. Cook slowly for 3/4 hr. in 1 qt. water. When tender, press through a puree sieve. Add hot milk. Blend butter, flour and a little bit of hot soup. Stir all together until smooth and thickened. Add parsley and cream. Can be served with souffle balls.

Cream of Pea Soup

1 qt. peas
1 c. cubed ham
1/2 c. ham broth

3 c. milk
1 tsp. salt
1 Tbsp. sugar

Cook peas and put through a strainer, reserving the water in which peas were cooked. Brown and cook ham until tender. Combine all ingredients and the water. Bring to a boil. If desired, add 1/2 c. cream before serving. Serve with crackers.

Spinach Soup

1 tsp. butter
1 1/2 c. chopped onion
1 qt. pureed spinach
1/2 tsp. garlic powder
1 tsp. salt

1/2 tsp. celery salt
Dash pepper
1 c. evaporated milk
1 pt. milk

In a saucepan melt butter. Sauté onion. Combine rest of ingredients and add onions. Bring to boiling point. Serves 12 - 14.

Elephant Soup

1 elephant (not too old)
15 gallons of brown gravy
10 lbs. of pepper

12 lbs. salt
1 rabbit

Cut elephant into small bite-sized pieces. That will take about 4 - 6 months. add salt and pepper and cover with brown gravy. Place concoction in a very large oven and cook at 700° for one week until tender.

This recipe will serve 3,800 to 4,500 persons. If more guests are expected, add the rabbit. Do that only if necessary, as most folks don't like a hare in their soup!

❧

A RECIPE FOR A DAY

Take a little dash of water cold,
    And a little leaven of prayer,
And a little bit of morning gold,
    Dissolved in the morning air.

Add to your meal some merriment,
    And a thought of kith and kin,
And then as your prime ingredient,
    A plenty of work thrown in.

But spice it all with the essence of love,
    And a little whiff of play,
Let a wise old book and a glance above
    Complete a well-made day.

Notes

Salads, Sandwiches and Drinks

ôŵ

The Beauty of Springtime

As we see the spring unfolding
  With its beauty and its flowers,
We are made to stop and wonder
  At the greatness of God's power.

How the changing seasons bless us
  With their beauty and their cheer;
How the God of love provides for,
  And takes care of His children here.

As the springtime comes upon us
  And the earth does resurrect;
Birds greet us with their chorus
  And flowers bloom as we'd expect.

We see these scenes of nature
  And think as we break the soil:
Earthly gain is least important
  As we consider our spiritual toil.

Dear Brethren, as we labor
  In the vineyard of the Lord,
Are we sowing seeds of goodness
  As is written in His Word?

We can plant them as we travel
  O'er the straight and narrow way.
For they're the only things that last
  In the light of Heaven's Day.

23

Chicken Salad

2 c. diced chicken
$1/2$ c. mayonnaise
$1/2$ tsp. pepper

$1/2$ tsp. salt
$1/2$ c. celery, chopped

Serve on fresh lettuce or in sandwich.

Broccoli Salad

1 head cauliflower
1 bundle broccoli, cut up

1 lb. bacon
1 pkg. shredded cheddar cheese

Dressing:
$1 1/2$ c. salad dressing
1 tsp. salt

$1 1/2$ c. white sugar
$1/2$ c. sweet-n-sour dressing

Run cauliflower through salad master. Fry bacon, drain and crumble. The dressing can be put on the day before but wait to add bacon and cheese until ready to serve.

Mother's Day Salad

1 head lettuce
$1/2$ c. onions
$1/2$ c. peppers
8 strips bacon

2 c. cheese
4 hard boiled eggs
$1/2$ c. frozen peas, optional

Dressing:
2 c. salad dressing
1 c. sugar

Little vinegar
Pinch of salt and pepper

Put lettuce in first, then onions, peppers and cheese. Add dressing. Top with hard boiled eggs, bacon and peas. Refrigerate overnight.

Potato Salad

3-4 lb. potatoes
1 c. diced celery

1 c. diced onions
1 doz. hard boiled eggs

Dressing:
  2 c. sugar
  1/2 c. vinegar or lemon juice
  5 eggs

1/2 tsp. salt
1 Tbsp. mustard
1 Tbsp. butter

Put all dressing ingredients in blender and mix. Pour into sauce pan and heat on medium till thickened or right below boiling point. Stir constantly. Remove from heat and cool 5 min. Beat in 2 c. Miracle Whip. Stir in potato mixture.

Cauliflower Salad

1 head lettuce, chunked
1 head cauliflower, sliced
1 chopped onion
1/4 - 1/2 c. Parmesan cheese

1 lb. bacon, fried and crumbled
2 c. salad dressing
1/2 c. sugar

  Mix well and chill.

Taco Salad

1 lb. hamburg
Tortilla chips
1 can kidney beans
1 c. sour cream
1 pkg. taco seasoning

Lettuce
Tomatoes
Peppers
Onions

Cheese sauce:
  1/4 c. butter
  1/2 lb. Velveeta cheese

3/4 c. sour cream

  Brown hamburg. Add taco seasoning. Mix and simmer according to package instructions. Layer bottom of platter with tortilla chips. Add hamburg and kidney beans. Spread with sour cream. Add lettuce, tomatoes, peppers and onions.

  To make cheese sauce: Melt butter and cheese together. Add sour cream and mix well. Pour over top of salad.

Apple Salad

2 eggs, beaten
2 Tbsp. flour
1 c. water

1 c. sugar
2 tsp. butter
1 tsp. vanilla

Boil all together and cool. When ready to use, add apples, bananas, raisins and nuts. Stir whipped topping into mixture for a fluffier texture, if you wish.

Jello Carrot Salad

1 box orange jello
1/2 c. finely grated carrots

1 c. crushed pineapple, optional

Mix according to directions on box, using slightly more water and 2 Tbsp. sugar. When jello starts to thicken, add carrots and pineapple. Stir and let set.

Sweetheart Salad

2 c. crushed pineapple
1/2 c. sugar
1/2 Tbsp. plain gelatin
1 c. cold water
8 oz. Philadelphia cream cheese

2 Tbsp. lemon juice
2 Tbsp. cherry juice
1 c. whipping cream
12 maraschino cherries

Dissolve gelatin in cold water. Add pineapple to sugar. Bring to boiling point and add gelatin. Stir until gelatin is dissolved. Add lemon and cherry juice. Cool. Mash cream cheese and add chopped cherries. Combine with pineapple mixture, adding a small amount at a time. Chill until slightly thickened. Whip cream and blend with salad mixture. Mold and chill.

Christmas Salad

1st Layer:
   $3^{1}/_{2}$ c. hot water
   $^{3}/_{4}$ c. lime jello
   1 can pineapple, drain and save juice

2nd Layer:
   1 c. pineapple juice
   $1^{1}/_{2}$ tsp. gelatin, dissolved
   3 oz. cream cheese
   1 pkg. Dream Whip

Cook the pineapple juice and add the dissolved gelatin. Remove and add the cream cheese. Chill, then add the Dream Whip.

3rd Layer:
   $3^{1}/_{2}$ c. boiling water
   $^{3}/_{4}$ c. strawberry jello

Yum-Yum Salad

1 can (13 oz.) evaporated milk
1 can (20 oz.) crushed pineapple
$^{1}/_{2}$ c. sugar

1 pkg. (3 oz.) gelatin, any flavor
1 pkg. (8 oz.) cream cheese

Chill milk overnight. Boil pineapple and juice with sugar slowly for 5 min. Add gelatin and stir until dissolved. Cool. Beat cream cheese with chilled milk until fluffy. Fold in pineapple and gelatin mixture. Pour into a mold and chill until firm.

Indiana Salad

1 c. lime jello
4 c. boiling water
1 lg. can crushed pineapple, drained
1 c. whipped cream
8 oz. Philadelphia cream cheese

Juice from pineapple
3/4 c. sugar
3 level Tbsp. flour
3 egg yolks
Pinch of salt

First Part: Mix jello. When starting to set, add pineapple and nuts.

Second Part: Mix together whipped cream and cream cheese. Mix until smooth and put on first part when set.

Third Part: Add sugar to juice of pineapple, then enough water to make 1 1/2 c. Stir flour into water. Add eggs and salt. Cook until smooth; cool and put on top.

Ritz Cracker Dip

2 eggs
3 Tbsp. sugar
2 Tbsp. vinegar
1/4 tsp. salt

8 oz. cream cheese
Chopped onion
Chopped green pepper

Beat eggs and sugar until thick. Add vinegar and salt. Place in double boiler over medium heat and stir until thick. Remove from heat and add cream cheese; beat until creamy. Add chopped onion and green pepper to taste. Refrigerate until chilled. Serve with Ritz crackers or potato chips.

Vegetable Dip

1 pt. sour cream
1 pkg. Hidden Valley Ranch mix
1/2 c. Miracle Whip

Mix all together. This can be kept in refrigerator for a week or more.

Cracker Dip

16 oz. soft cream cheese
16 oz. sour cream
1 1/2 c. granulated sugar

1 tsp. vinegar
Pinch of salt
1 pkg. Hidden Valley Ranch mix

Mix and serve.

Spam Burgers

1 can Spam, ground
2 tsp. minced onion
1/2 lb. sharp cheddar cheese, grated

3 Tbsp. milk
2 Tbsp. mayonnaise
2 Tbsp. pickled relish

Mix all ingredients together, then put on top of buns. Bake at 350° till cheese melts.

Ham Salad Sandwiches

2 c. ground, cooked ham
3 stalks celery
1 lg. dill pickle
1/4 tsp. dry mustard

1/4 tsp. onion powder
1/2 c. mayonnaise
1/2 tsp. salt
1 Tbsp. lemon juice

Put ham, celery and pickle through coarse blade of food chopper. Add remaining ingredients and mix.

Sloppy Joe Sandwiches

2 Tbsp. fat
1 lb. hamburger
2 mod. onions, chopped
1 tsp. salt
1/8 tsp. pepper

1 Tbsp. flour
1 c. water
1/2 tsp. Worcestershire sauce
3/4 c. catsup
10 sandwich buns

Melt fat in skillet. Add hamburger, onions, salt and pepper. Cook until meat is lightly browned, stirring occasionally. Blend flour and water, pour into meat, mixing well. Add Worcestershire sauce and catsup, simmer, stirring occasionally for 15 - 20 min. until desired consistency is obtained. Serve on warmed sandwich buns.

Quick Root Beer

2 c. sugar
1 gal. water

4 tsp. root beer
1 tsp. yeast

Set in sun 4 hrs. Chill and serve.

Lemonade

6 lemons
1 1/2 c. sugar

2 1/2 qt. water

Slice lemons in thin rings. Add sugar and pound to extract juice. Let stand 20 min. and then add cold water and ice cubes. Stir until well blended. Makes 3 qt.

Homemade Lemonade

1 c. squeezed lemons
2 c. sugar

1 gal. water
Plenty of ice cubes

Add sugar to lemons then add water and ice. Stir until well blended. Makes 1 gal.

Tomato Juice

8 qt. tomatoes, cut up
2 bunches celery
3 green peppers
1 bunch parsley

6 sm. onions
1 c. sugar
1/2 tsp. paprika
1 tsp. salt to each qt.

Boil tomatoes, celery, parsley, onions and peppers together. Run through food mill. Add sugar, salt and paprika. Bring to boil and seal.

Wedding Punch

2 1/2 c. pineapple juice, chilled
1 pt. lime, lemon or raspberry sherbet

1 pt. vanilla ice cream
12 oz. ginger ale or 7-Up

Combine pineapple juice, sherbet and 1 c. ice cream. Beat until smooth. Add 7-Up or ginger ale. Spoon remaining ice cream into punch. Serve immediately.

Ice Cream Punch

1 qt. frozen orange concentrate
2 qt. water

2 qt. ginger ale
1 qt. vanilla ice cream

Mix all ingredients and chill.

Hot Chocolate

$1/2$ c. cocoa
1 c. sugar

Dash of salt
$2/3$ c. water

Boil this together then add 2 qt. of milk or to suit your taste. This same recipe can be used for cold chocolate milk. Just cool the syrup then add ice cold milk.

Grape Juice

8 qt. grapes
2 qt. water
2 lb. sugar

Add water to grapes and boil 10 min. Strain through a cloth bag. Add sugar, boil 10 min. and seal.

Grape Juice

Wash fully ripened Concord grapes and spoon into a qt. jar until it is ⅓ full. Add ½ c. sugar and water to fill the jar. Seal and boil for 10 min. Strain the juice and add plenty of ice cubes before serving. Delicious!

Tea Concentrate to Freeze

4 qt. water
4 qt. sugar
4 c. tea leaves (packed full)

Bring water to a full boil, then add tea leaves and let set for 20 min. Put through sieve then add sugar. Put in boxes and freeze. When ready to serve mix 1 part frozen concentrate to 3 parts water. Suit your own taste.

When at night you sleepless lie
    and the weary hours drag by
Lift your thoughts to God above,
    bending down to you in Love.
Feel His presence by your bed.
His soft touch upon your head.
Let your last thought be a prayer,
    as you nestle in His care.
Ask Him all your way to keep,
    then, O then, drop off to sleep.

Meats and Vegetables

ૐ

Cleaning Cupboards

Today while cleaning cupboards
   With neat, housewifely art
I suddenly decided
   To clean the cupboards of my heart.

I threw out criticism
   To the trashpile – to the fire!
I put in appreciation
   And worthwhile thoughts that inspire.

I threw out condemnations
   Which says, you're wrong, I'm right!
I put in consideration
   For all folks, brown, black and white.

Yes, out went complaining
   Grumbling about trivial things
I put in smiles and laughter.
   To ease the tensions each day brings.

Friends, let's all clean our cupboards,
   With help from God above
Throw out pride and hatred, too.
   Put in humility and love.

Roast
(Thanksgiving Dinner)

16 lb. turkey
4 loaves bread
9 eggs
3 qt. chopped celery

1 med. onion, chopped
1 lb. butter
1/2 lb. margarine

Cube bread and beat eggs. Mix together. Then add celery and onions and simmer a little. Brown butter then melt margarine in butter. Mix all ingredients together and stuff turkey. Bake for 4 - 5 hrs. Bake rest of filling separately. Or pick all the meat off roasted turkey and mix with filling, baking for another hr. at 350°, stirring occasionally. Serve with mashed potatoes, cooked celery and coleslaw.

Deer Meat Roast

Venison roast
3 Tbsp. bacon fat
1/2 c. vinegar
1 c. water
Salt to taste

Kitchen Bouquet
1 med. onion, diced
2 tsp. cornstarch
1/2 - 2/3 c. water

Marinate the venison overnight in vinegar and water. Turn once. Before cooking, drain liquid. Pat meat dry and season to taste with salt and Kitchen Bouquet. Brown in bacon fat with onion. Put in oven set at 350°. Bake same amount of time as a beef roast of like size. Baste often, add carrots and celery the last hr. Use cornstarch and water to thicken gravy.

Poor Man's Steak

1 1/2 lb. hamburger
1/4 tsp. pepper
1 c. cracker crumbs

1 sm. onion, chopped
1 c. milk
1 tsp. salt

Mix all ingredients well and shape into a meatloaf. Let set 8 hrs. Then cut into 1" slices and fry on both sides in oil. Layer the slices in a roast pan and spread 1 can cream of mushroom soup over all the meat. Bake one hour at 325°.

Quick Cheeseburger Bake

1 lb. ground beef
1 can cheddar cheese soup
1 c. frozen mixed vegetables, optional
1/4 c. milk

3/4 c. water
1 c. shredded cheddar cheese
3/4 c. chopped onion
2 c. bisquick

Heat oven to 400°. Grease 13" x 9" baking dish. Cook beef and onion in skillet until beef is brown, drain then stir in soup, vegetables and milk. Stir together bisquick and water in bowl until moistened. Spread evenly in baking dish. Spread beef mixture and vegetables over batter and spread with cheese. Bake 30 min.

Barbequed Meatballs

2 lbs. ground beef
1 c. oatmeal
2 eggs
1/2 tsp. salt
2 tsp. chili

1 c. evap. milk
1 c. cracker crumbs
1/2 c. chopped onions
1/2 tsp. pepper

Mix well and roll into balls. Put in cake pan.

Sauce:
2 c. catsup
1/2 tsp. liquid smoke
1/4 c. chopped onion

1 c. brown sugar
1/2 tsp. garlic powder

Mix and pour over meatballs. Bake at 350° for 45 min.

Sale, Barbeque Recipe

1 Tbsp. chopped onions
1 lb. hamburger
Dash of salt and pepper
1/2 c. catsup

1 Tbsp. vinegar
1 Tbsp. sugar
1 Tbsp. Worcestershire sauce

Fry together onions, hamburger, salt and pepper until lightly browned. Mix rest of ingredients together. Add to hamburger mixture and mix well. Let simmer for 10 - 15 min. If this seems plenty strong use less catsup and add some tomato juice.

Glazed Meat Loaf

1½ lb. ground hamburger
1 c. 100% All Bran cereal
½ c. chopped onion
⅓ c. ketchup
¼ c. water

2 eggs, beaten
1½ tsp. Worchestershire sauce
1¼ tsp. salt
¼ tsp. black pepper

Glaze:
1 Tbsp. ketchup
1 Tbsp. honey or dark corn syrup

¼ tsp. Worchestershire sauce

Mix ingredients for meat loaf. Shape as a loaf and place in a baking dish. Cover and bake at 375° for 40 min. Mix glaze in a small bowl. Remove lid and brush top with glaze. Leave uncovered and bake 10 more min. Serves 6.

Beef Barbecue for Canning

10 lb. ground beef
5 c. chopped onions
¼ c. salt (scant)
1¼ Tbsp. pepper
1 c. vinegar

¾ c. prepared mustard
1½ c. brown sugar
⅔ c. Worchestershire sauce
5 c. catsup

Brown hamburg and onions. Add the other ingredients and 4 c. beef broth or water, (or more if necessary). Steam 10 min. Pack in jars and seal. Makes about 9 qt. Boil 1 - 2 hrs.

A Recipe to Live By

Blend 1 c. of love and ½ c. of kindness. Add alternately in small portions, 1 c. of appreciation and 3 c. of pleasant companionship, into which has been sifted 3 tsp. of deserving praise. Flavor with 1 tsp. carefully chosen advice. Fold in 1 c. of cheerfulness to which has been added a pinch of sorrow. Pour with tender care into small clean hearts and bake until well matured. Turn out on the surface of society, humbly invoke God's blessings and it will serve all mankind. ❧

Corned Beef

50 lbs. beef (roasts, steaks or any choice cut)
3 qt. salt

Place meat in a large crock or similar suitable container and add salt alternately. Let stand overnight. Then rinse off roughly and pack in crock again.

Make a brine of:
1/4 lb. baking soda	2 lbs. brown sugar
1/4 lb. salt petre	2 Tbsp. liquid smoke
Enough water to cover meat	

This meat will be cured for use in 2 weeks. It can then be cut in suitable pieces and canned (cold pack 3 hrs.) or put in freezer. If crock is kept in a cool place, meat may be kept in brine and used anytime within 3 months.

Baked Ham

3 or 4 slices ham (3/4")	4 Tbsp. brown sugar
2 Tbsp. dry mustard	Milk

Place ham slices in roast pan. Rub dry mustard and brown sugar over top. Add barely enough milk to cover. Bake at 350° for 1 - 1 1/2 hrs. This is delicious!

Mock Ham Loaf

1 lb. hamburger	1 tsp. salt
1/2 lb. hot dogs, ground fine	Dash of pepper
1 c. cracker crumbs	1 egg

Combine all ingredients. Add half of the glaze mixture to ingredients. Mix well. Shape into a loaf. Bake at 350° for 1 1/2 hrs. Baste occasionally with the glaze.

Glaze:
3/4 c. brown sugar	1/2 tsp. mustard
1/2 c. water	1 Tbsp. vinegar

Mock Turkey Loaf

1 lb. ground turkey
½ lb. ground hot dogs
1 c. cracker crumbs

1 beaten egg
Salt and pepper to taste

Mix above ingredients together.

Sauce:
    ¾ c. brown sugar
    ½ c. water

½ tsp. dry mustard
1 Tbsp. vinegar

Mix half the sauce into the meat mixture and shape into a loaf. Pour the rest of the sauce over top. Bake at 325° for 1 hr.

Chili

1 lb. hamburger
½ c. brown sugar
2 Tbsp. table mustard
1 med. onion, chopped
2 14-oz. cans kidney beans

1 pt. tomato juice
½ tsp. salt
¼ tsp. pepper
2 tsp. chili powder

Brown first four ingredients. Add everything else and simmer for 1 hr.

Chicken Croquettes

2 c. ground chicken
⅛ tsp. pepper
½ tsp. celery salt

½ tsp. salt
¼ tsp. onion salt

White Sauce:
    2 Tbsp. butter
    1 c. milk

2½ Tbsp. flour

Make the white sauce by bringing these 3 ingredients to a boil. Cool sauce, then add to chicken and seasoning. Shape into patties and roll into beaten eggs and then coat with cracker crumbs. These can be baked or fried.

Chicken Pie

1 Tbsp. butter
3 Tbsp. flour
1 qt. chicken broth
1 c. cooked chicken, cut up

1 c. cooked potatoes, cut fine
1 c. cooked celery
1½ c. cooked carrots
3 hard boiled eggs

Dough:
2 c. flour
½ c. milk
2 level Tbsp. lard

1½ tsp. baking powder
Salt to taste

Put butter into baking dish. Melt and mix with flour. Cook until creamy. Add rest of ingredients. Cover top with dough. Bake in moderate oven.

Chicken Pot Pie

Dough:
2 c. flour
½ tsp. salt

2 eggs
2 - 3 Tbsp. water

Make a well in the flour and add the eggs and salt. Work together into a stiff dough. If too dry, add water or milk. Roll out the dough as thin as possible (⅛") and cut in 1" squares with a knife or pastry wheel. Drop into the boiling broth.

Pot Pie:
1 chicken, 4 lb. preferably a hen
1 tsp. salt

4 med. potatoes, sliced
2 Tbsp. minced parsley

Cut chicken into serving pieces, cover with water and cook until tender. Season with salt when chicken is almost soft and add the sliced potatoes and squares of pot pie dough and cook 20 min. longer. Add chopped parsley.

Old Fashioned Pot Pie

2 eggs
$\frac{1}{2}$ c. milk
1 tsp. salt
Flour to make stiff dough or nice to roll

2 med. potatoes, peeled
1$\frac{1}{2}$ qt. broth, chicken or beef

Dice potatoes in broth, when it starts to boil add dough, which has been rolled thin and cut in small squares. Add each square separately and keep cooking while adding. When all the squares are added cook for 10 - 15 min. Stir. Add cooked beef or chicken. Bring to a boil, then serve.

Turkey Pie

4 potatoes
2 c. carrots
2 c. peas
$\frac{1}{2}$ c. onion

$\frac{1}{4}$ c. flour
1$\frac{1}{2}$ c. water
2 Tbsp. butter
3 c. diced turkey

Cook vegetables in a little water until done. Then add the sauce made of water, flour and butter cooked together. Also mix the chicken with sauce and vegetables. Use as a pie filling.

Pie Crust:
2 c. flour
$\frac{2}{3}$ c. shortening

Pinch of salt
Little water

Bake pies at 400° for 10 min., then 20 min. at 350°. Makes 3 8" pies. When ready to eat pour a good rich gravy over your piece of pie.

Meal In One

1 round steak
5 med. potatoes

2 sm. onions, sliced
1 can mushroom soup

Place steak in casserole dish. Place sliced (pared) potatoes on top of steak. Next, put sliced onions on top of potatoes. Pour soup over all. Salt and pepper to taste. Add carrots if desired. Bake at 375° for 2 hrs.

Baked Liver

1 lb. thinly sliced liver   Salt and pepper to taste

Dip liver in flour. Brown in frying pan, then place in casserole dish.

Sauce:
1 lg. onion, chopped $1/2$ c. ketchup
1 Tbsp. butter   2 Tbsp. vinegar
2 tsp. dry mustard $1/2$ c. water
4 tsp. sugar

Cook sauce 10 min. Pour over liver and bake at 350° for 1 hr.

Fried Oysters

3 doz. oysters $1/2$ tsp. salt
2 eggs, beaten   1 Tbsp. water
$1/2$ c. fine cracker crumbs

Drain oysters. Dip in seasoned crumbs, egg diluted with water and then in crumbs again. Fry with butter until golden brown.

Dried Beef

$4^1/2$ gal. water   20 lb. beef
Enough salt to float an egg   2 lb. brown sugar
1 oz. salt petre

Put weight on top to keep meat in brine. For large pieces soak 60 hrs., small pieces 48 hrs.

Steak Bar-B-Que Sauce

1 sm. onion, minced
2 Tbsp. cooking oil
1 Tbsp. mustard
2 Tbsp. sugar
Few drops Tabasco sauce

2 Tbsp. Worcestershire sauce
2 Tbsp. vinegar
1 can tomato paste
1/4 c. catsup

Brush this on steak as you barbecue it. This sauce is good on spare ribs and other pork.

Chicken Bar-B-Que Mix
(To make over charcoal)

6 c. vinegar
1 c. salt

3 c. Mazola corn oil
4 c. boiling water

Shake salt and vinegar together very well until salt dissolves. Add oil and water. Put in sprayer and shake well each time before you spray chicken. This should be enough for 40 lbs. of chicken. Also sprinkle a generous amount of pepper on chicken while still on grill.

Bar-B-Q Sauce for Chicken

3/4 c. oleo
2 tsp. paprika
1 tsp. sugar
1 tsp. salt
1/2 tsp. pepper

1/4 tsp. dry mustard
1/2 tsp. lemon juice
1/2 c. hot water
Few drops Worcestershire sauce

Combine all ingredients thoroughly and spread over chicken. Bake 1 1/2 hr. at 350°.

Meat Cure

2 lb. brown sugar
4 gal. water
6 lb. salt

2 oz. pepper
1 oz. salt petre

Bring to a boil, then cool. Pack meat in tub or crock as tightly as possible. Put weight on top to keep meat in brine. Leave hams in 4 weeks, bacon only 5 - 6 days. Then smoke, and wrap in paper or cloth.

Sugar Meat Cure
(For a 200 lb. hog)

2 qt. salt
1 qt. brown sugar

1 Tbsp. pepper
1 tsp. salt petre

Dissolve salt petre in a little water. Rub meat well with this mix. Let lay for 12 days. Then hang it up and smoke.

Smoke Brine for Turkey

Put turkey in crock and cover with the following:

$1/4$ lb. Morton's Tender Quick
3 Tbsp. liquid smoke
1 gal. water

Cover and let stand 24 hrs. Then cook as usual for a turkey.

Potluck Potatoes

2 sticks butter
2 pt. sour cream
2 cans cream of chicken soup
1 lb. Velveeta

1/2 tsp. pepper
1 tsp. seasoned salt
2 tsp. salt
4 lb. frozen hash browns

Mix all together and put into roaster. Crush 5 - 6 c. corn flakes and mix with 2 sticks browned butter. Put on top. Bake at 350° for 1 hr.

Potato Kugel

4 c. potatoes, cubed, uncooked
3 eggs
1 lg. onion, quartered
1 1/2 tsp. salt

1/4 tsp. pepper
1/4 c. chicken fat or butter, melted
1/3 c. potato flour or all purpose flour
6 sprigs parsley

Heat oven to 350°. Grease a 1 1/2 qt. casserole. Blender-grate potatoes in cold water in blender. Drain well. Put remaining ingredients into blender and process until parsley is chopped. Mix batter thoroughly with potatoes and pour into greased casserole. Bake at 350° for 1 hr. or until brown. 1 c. ham cut in cubes may be added.

Potato Filling

4 lg. potatoes, mashed
4 slices bread, diced
1 c. milk
1/4 c. onions, diced

2 Tbsp. chopped celery
3 Tbsp. butter
1 tsp. salt
Dash of pepper

Mix mashed potatoes with diced bread. Heat milk and beat into potatoes and bread. Sauté onion and celery in butter until golden brown. Add to potatoes with salt and pepper. Mix well; put into a greased 2 qt. casserole and bake at 350° for 45 min.

Gourmet Potatoes

6 med. potatoes
1 c. shredded cheese
1/4 c. butter
1/2 c. chopped onions
1 1/2 c. sour milk

1 tsp. salt
1/4 tsp. pepper
2 Tbsp. butter
1 Tbsp. paprika

Cook potatoes and grate. Combine cheese and butter until melted. Remove from heat. Stir in sour cream, salt and pepper. Put into a 2 qt. casserole. Dot with butter and paprika. Bake at 350° for 30 min. uncovered.

Potato Cheese Pie

Crust:
 2 - 2 1/2 c. mashed potatoes
 2 Tbsp. flour
 1 tsp. baking powder

1 egg
2 Tbsp. melted butter
Salt and pepper

Filling:
 2 eggs
 1 c. sour cream

Salt and pepper
3/4 c. grated Velveeta cheese

Mix the crust ingredients thoroughly and pat into a large greased pie plate as if dough. Beat the eggs, stir in cream and seasonings. Pour this into the potato crust and sprinkle the top with cheese. Bake at 350° for 20 min. or until an inserted knife comes out clean.

Potato Puffs

1 c. mashed potatoes
1 - 2 beaten eggs
1/4 tsp. salt

1/4 - 1/2 c. flour
1 tsp. baking powder

Mix well and drop by teaspoon in deep lard. Fry until brown on both sides.

Baked Sweet Potatoes

5 med. sweet potatoes
1 tsp. salt
¾ c. brown sugar
2 Tbsp. butter

3 Tbsp. flour
8 marshmallows
1 c. thin cream

Cook potatoes until tender. Drain and cool slightly. Cut potatoes in half lengthwise and put in baking dish. Mix salt, sugar and flour and pour over potatoes. Dot with butter and marshmallows and pour the cream over top. Bake at 350° for 45 - 50 min.

Sweet Potato Patties

2 c. cooked and mashed sweet potatoes
½ c. brown sugar
1 tsp. salt

Form into small patties and roll into Saltine cracker crumbs. Fry in a pan with plenty of butter until nicely browned.

Baked Corn

2 c. corn
1½ Tbsp. flour
1 c. milk
½ tsp. pepper

2 eggs
½ c. butter
2 c. bread cubes
Sugar, optional

Mix corn, flour, milk, pepper and beaten eggs. Put in casserole. Melt butter, then add bread cubes. Spread over top. Bake at 350° for 1 hr.

Corn Fritters

1 c. creamed corn
1 c. whole kernel corn
1 c. cracker crumbs
1 Tbsp. sugar
1 tsp. salt

2 eggs
1½ tsp. baking powder
Pinch of pepper
1 Tbsp. butter

Mix all ingredients together. If batter seems thin add ½ c. flour. Deep fat fry until golden brown.

Lena's Zucchini Casserole

1 lg. shredded zucchini
3 shredded potatoes
2 c. sausage or hamburger

Salt and pepper to taste
Shredded cheese
2 - 3 tomatoes

Mix and put in pan. Slice tomatoes on top. If desired tomatoes can also be chopped and added to mixture. Bake in 350° oven for 1 hr.

Zucchini Casserole

4 c. grated zucchini
⅓ c. vegetable oil
½ tsp. garlic powder
1 Tbsp. parsley flakes

1 c. bisquick
½ c. grated cheese
4 eggs, beaten

Mix all ingredients together. Put in casserole and bake at 350° for approximately 50 min.

Zucchini Loaf

1 c. biscuit mix
1/2 c. oil
1/2 c. Cheez Whiz or Velveeta
1/2 tsp. garlic powder

1/2 tsp. salt
4 eggs
3 c. grated zucchini

Mix all ingredients then pour mixture into greased casserole and bake at 350° for 45 min. or until set.

String Bean Casserole

Make layers of canned string beans and onion rings. Add celery or mushroom soup. Top with buttered bread crumbs. Bake at 350° for 1 hr.

Tomato Casserole

Tomatoes
Pepper rings
Onion rings

Sugar
Salt and pepper
Bread crumbs

Slice raw tomatoes into a cake pan. Over these arrange pepper and onion rings. Season with sugar, salt and pepper. Cover with bread crumbs, seasoned with salt, pepper and butter as for filling. Bake in moderate oven 1 - 1 1/2 hrs.

Baked Stuffed Tomatoes

6 lg. tomatoes
1/2 tsp. salt
1 egg, well beaten
1 tsp. minced parsley

1 c. bread crumbs
1 Tbsp. minced onion
2 Tbsp. melted butter

Remove stems from tomatoes and cut out centers. Fill with filling made from the rest of the ingredients. Place in a baking dish and bake in a 375° (moderately hot) oven for 30 min.

Barbecued Lima Beans

2 c. lima beans
2 Tbsp. butter
1 med. onion
2 Tbsp. flour

2 Tbsp. brown sugar
1 Tbsp. vinegar
1 c. canned, whole tomatoes
$1/2$ c. tomato juice

Fry onion in butter. Add vinegar, sugar and flour. Mix well and add rest of ingredients. Ham or bacon can also be added. Cook limas 5 - 10 min. Add to sauce. Bake at 350° for 30 min.

Creamed Celery

1 qt. finely cut celery
$1/2$ tsp. salt

$1/2$ c. sugar
2 Tbsp. vinegar

Cook together until tender, not using more water than necessary. Add a sauce made with 1 Tbsp. flour and a little milk. Bring to a boil, then stir in 2 Tbsp. salad dressing or mayonnaise.

Cooked Celery

2 qt. celery
1 tsp. salt
1 c. water
$1/2$ c. sugar
Butter (size of walnut)

2 tsp. vinegar
$1/2$ c. milk
$2^1/2$ Tbsp. brown sugar
2 Tbsp. flour

Boil the celery, salt, water, sugar and butter until soft, then add rest of ingredients. Bring to a boil, then serve.

Stuffed Cabbage

1 lg. head cabbage
2 lb. hamburger
½ c. rice, cooked

2 egg
2 cans tomato soup

Core cabbage and bring the water to a boil with the whole head of cabbage. Pour off water. Cool cabbage. Mix hamburger, rice and eggs. Carefully remove cabbage leaves and roll hamburger mixture into each leaf. Put in large pot. Add diluted tomato soup. Cook for 2 hrs. on low heat. Makes about 20 rolls.

Asparagus and Bread Dish

Bread
4 eggs
2 c. milk
Salt and pepper

Onion, to taste
2½ c. cooked asparagus
Cheese

Layer slices of bread in bottom of a 9" x 9" pan. Beat eggs with milk, salt, pepper, and onion and pour over bread. Bake 25 min. Add the asparagus and put sliced cheese on top of asparagus and bake another 10 min.

Crisp Baked Eggplant

Peel and slice rounds of eggplant about ½" thick. Dip in flour, milk, flour, then milk again. Then coat with plain or seasoned bread crumbs. Place each slice on a cookie sheet with 1 Tbsp. oleo under each slice. Put 1 tsp. oleo on top of each slice. Bake at 350° for 30 - 40 min. turning once during cooking. The outsides are crunchy, insides soft and delicious. We also slice unpeeled eggplant, use Italian dressing and grill.

White Sauce

Thin(1 1/2 c.):
    1 Tbsp. butter   1/2 tsp. salt
    1 Tbsp. flour   1 1/2 c. milk

Medium (1 c.)
    2 Tbsp. butter   1/4 tsp. salt
    2 Tbsp. flour   1 c. milk

Thick (1 c.)
    3 Tbsp. butter   1/4 tsp. salt
    4 Tbsp. flour   1 c. milk

Melt butter in saucepan over low heat. Blend in flour, salt and a dash of white pepper. Add milk all at once. Cook quickly, stirring constantly, till mixture thickens and bubbles.

3 Minute Cheese Sauce

1 2/3 c. undiluted Carnation evaporated milk
1/2 tsp. salt
1 c. grated American cheese

Heat Carnation milk and salt in saucepan over low heat to just below boiling. Add cheese. Continue heating until cheese melts. Use on beans or pour over cooked potatoes.

Tomato Sauce

2 Tbsp. shortening   1/8 tsp. pepper
1/3 c. flour   1 tsp. salt
3/4 c. milk   1 1/2 c. grated Velveeta cheese
2 1/2 c. stewed fresh tomatoes or
    canned tomatoes

Melt shortening in a saucepan over low heat. Blend in flour. Stir in milk, tomatoes and seasonings and cook until slightly thickened, stirring often. Mix in grated cheese. Serve on crisp toast, crackers or potatoes.

Schnitz Un Knepp

3 lb. ham
1 qt. dried apples
2 Tbsp. brown sugar
2 c. flour
4 tsp. baking powder
Milk (enough to make a fairly moist stiff batter)

1/4 tsp. pepper
1 egg, well beaten
3 Tbsp. melted butter
1 tsp. salt

Wash dried apples. Cover with water and soak overnight. Cover ham with boiling water and boil 3 hrs. Add apples and water in which they were soaked and boil 1 hr. longer. Add sugar.

Make dumplings by sifting flour, salt, pepper and baking powder. Stir in beaten egg, milk and shortening. Drop by tablespoons into hot ham and apples. Cover and cook 15 min. Serve hot.

Hay Stacks

Ritz crackers
Sloppy joe mixture
    (prepared as for sandwiches)
Lettuce, cut-up
Carrots, grated

Celery, cut fine
2 cans cheddar cheese soup
    diluted with 1 1/2 cans milk
Tomatoes, cut up
Onions, chopped

Break up Ritz crackers on plates. Spread a layer of sloppy joe mixture over crackers, then a layer of each of the cut-up vegetables. Heat the cheddar cheese soup and milk and pour over the top of the vegetables. Your favorite salad dressing may be added last or it may be eaten without the dressing.

Baked Lasagna

1 pkg. lasagna noodles
1 lb. ground beef
1/3 c. onions, chopped
1 Tbsp. parsley
1 tsp. salt

1/8 tsp. pepper
3 cans (8 oz. each) tomato sauce
1 1/2 c. white American cheese
1/2 c. grated Parmesan cheese

Cook noodles as directed on box and drain. In a large skillet brown meat, onions, parsley, salt and pepper. Add tomato sauce and simmer 10 min. Spoon some of sauce into a 9" x 13" greased cake pan and layer half the noodles, cheese and sauce. Repeat layering, ending with sauce. Bake at 375° for 30 min.

Stuffed Jumbo Shells

20-24 (8 oz.) jumbo macaroni shells
1 egg, beaten
3/4 c. soft bread crumbs
1/4 c. parsley (snipped)
1 Tbsp. onion

1/2 tsp. salt
1 lb. lean ground beef
3 c. favorite spaghetti or meat
  sauce (I use more)
1 c. mozzarella cheese, shredded

Cook shells in boiling water according to directions, drain. In mixing bowl combine egg, bread crumbs, parsley, onion and salt. Add meat and cheese. Mix well. Stuff shells. Pour 1/2 c. sauce in bottom of a 13" x 9" x 2" pan. Arrange shells on sauce and pour remaining sauce over top. Bake (uncovered) 1 1/4 hrs. at 375°. Different and good! These shells can be stuffed and spread out on trays to freeze. After they're frozen, store in plastic bags until ready to serve.

Delicious Leftover Casserole

Mix any kind of vegetables, rice, noodles, meat and gravy together. Put 5 slices of Velveeta cheese on top. Then put on topping consisting of:

3 c. cubed bread
1/3 c. melted butter
1 well beaten egg

Mix and season with salt, pepper and celery leaves. Bake 1 hr. at 350°.

Egg Cakes

7 eggs
2 Tbsp. flour

3/4 c. milk
1/2 tsp. salt

Beat eggs very well. Add flour and milk. Beat again. Brown 2 Tbsp. butter in 2 9" pie plates then pour mixture in plates and bake at 375° for 45 in. Serve with chicken and a vegetable.

Home Made Scrapple

2¾ c. water
¾ tsp. salt

1 c. cornmeal
¾ lb. pork puddens

Puddens is the heart, liver and scrap meats of pork, cooked and put through a grinder then cooked again with salt and pepper added. Heat water and salt to a boil. In separate bowl mix cornmeal with cold water till smooth then pour into hot water and stir to a boil. Cover and cook on low burner for 30 min. Stir occasionally. Add puddens the last 10 min. Blend then pour into a bread pan. Cool thoroughly. Slice and fry in a little vegetable oil till crisp and brown on each side.

Waffles

2 c. flour
2 tsp. baking powder
5 Tbsp. butter

¼ tsp. salt
3 eggs
1½ c. milk

Sift flour, then measure. Add other dry ingredients. Sift 3 times. To the well beaten egg yolks, add flour mixture with milk. Add butter which has been melted. Fold in egg whites and bake in waffle iron. Serve with chicken and gravy.

A Recipe for Making Lard

To a kettle of fat add:

3 Tbsp. soda
5 med. potatoes, peeled and sliced

Fry out as usual. This is to make a nicer, whiter lard and keeps it from getting a strong taste so soon.

Cakes

ᴥ

A Love Cake for Mother

1 c. obedience
Several lbs. affection
1 c. pure thoughtfulness
1 box powdered (willing) get up when I should
Some holidays, birthday and everyday surprises
1 bottle "Keep sunny all day long"
1 c. running errands
1 qt. neatness

Mix well and bake in a hearty warm oven and serve to Mother everyday. She likes it in big slices!

ᴥ

True Love

True love is but a humble, low-born thing
   And hath its food served up in earthenware;
It is a thing to walk with, hand in hand,
   Through the everydayness of this work-day world.
Baring its tender feet to every roughness,
   Yet letting not one heart-beat go astray
From beauty's law of plainness and content
   A simple fireside thing, whose quiet smile
Can warm earth's poorest hovel to a home.

Moist Chocolate Cake

2 1/4 c. flour
2 c. brown sugar
1/3 c. cocoa
2 tsp. baking soda
1 tsp. baking powder

1 tsp. salt
1/2 c. Wesson oil
1 c. ready to drink coffee
1 c. milk
2 eggs

Put in mixing bowl in order given then beat very well. Bake at 350° for 40 min.

Chocolate Sheet Cake

2 c. flour
2 c. sugar
1/2 c. oleo
4 Tbsp. cocoa
1/2 c. Crisco
1 c. water

2 beaten eggs
1/2 c. buttermilk or sour milk
1 tsp. soda
1 tsp. vanilla
1/4 tsp. salt

Put flour and sugar in large bowl and mix well. Mix and melt together oleo, cocoa and Crisco. Add 1 c. water and boil. Pour over flour and sugar mixture. Add rest of ingredients. Pour on greased cookie sheet and bake at 350°.

Frosting:
1/2 c. oleo
6 Tbsp. milk

4 Tbsp. cocoa
1 lb. powdered sugar

Bring to boil oleo, milk, cocoa. Pour over 1 lb. powdered sugar, beat well and add nuts if desired. A delicious sheet cake.

Chocolate Chip Cake

1/4 lb. soft butter
1 c. granulated sugar
2 eggs
1 tsp. vanilla

1 c. sour cream
2 c. flour
1 1/2 tsp. baking powder
1 tsp. baking soda

Mix in order given then beat well for 5 min. Pour in a 9" x 13" cake pan. Sprinkle 1/2 c. granulated sugar and 1 tsp. cinnamon over top and then 6 oz. chocolate chips. Bake at 350° for 30 min.

Chocolate Jelly Roll

5 egg yolks, beaten
1 c. 10x sugar
1/4 c. fine flour, sifted
5 stiffly beaten egg whites

1/2 tsp. salt
3 Tbsp. cocoa
1 tsp. vanilla

Add egg whites last and fold lightly to rest of ingredients. Bake at 350° for 10 - 12 min. Dump on lightly (10x) sugared cloth.

Filling:
1 c. milk
1 Tbsp. cornstarch
1/2 c. Crisco

1/4 c. butter
1 c. 10x sugar

Boil the milk and cornstarch and stir until thickened. Cool. Cream the Crisco, butter and 10x sugar. Add cornstarch mixture to Crisco mixture one teaspoon at a time and beat until fluffy.

Cowboy Cake

1 c. shortening
2 c. brown sugar
1 egg
1 c. thick milk (may use milk with 1 Tbsp. vinegar added)

1 tsp. cinnamon
1 tsp. soda
2 1/2 c. flour

Mix shortening, sugar and eggs, then add milk, flour, and spices.

Crumbs:
1/3 c. brown sugar
1/2 c. flour
1 Tbsp. butter

Mix ingredients together to form crumbs. Place crumbs on top of cake before baking. Bake at 350° for 45 min. or until toothpick comes out clean.

Best Ever Cake

1 c. shortening
2 c. brown sugar
2 eggs
1 Tbsp. vinegar
2½ c. flour

2 tsp. soda
½ tsp. salt
1 tsp. vanilla
½ c. cocoa
1 c. hot water

Mix ingredients in order given and pour into 9" x 13" pan. Bake at 350° for 40 - 45 min.

Angel Food Cake

1½ c. egg whites
1½ c. white sugar
1½ tsp. cream of tartar

1 c. cake flour
½ tsp. salt
1 tsp. almond flavoring

Sift together ¾ c. of the sugar and the flour 3 times. Set aside. Beat egg whites until frothy. Add salt and cream of tartar. Beat until it stand in peaks. Add ¾ c. of the sugar, about 3 Tbsp. at a time, beating well with eggbeater each time, after adding the sugar. Lightly fold in the sugar-flour mixture, adding about ½ c. at a time. Add flavoring. Bake at 375° for about 35 - 40 min.

Sour Cream Spice Cake

½ c. shortening
2 c. brown sugar
3 egg yolks, beaten
1 c. sour cream
1 tsp. vanilla
1 tsp. soda

2 tsp. cinnamon
1 tsp. cloves
1 tsp. allspice
1¾ c. flour sifted with
½ tsp. salt

Cream shortening, add sugar and cream well. Add flour, soda and spices. Add sour cream and beat well. Add vanilla and fold in stiffly beaten egg whites. Bake in greased 8" layer pans 25 min. at 350°.

Spice Cake

½ c. butter
2 c. light brown sugar
1 egg or 2 egg yolks (beaten light)
1 c. sour milk
2¼ c. sifted flour

1 tsp. soda
½ tsp. cinnamon
½ tsp. cloves
¼ tsp. nutmeg

Cream butter. Add sugar gradually, and egg yolks. Sift dry ingredients. Add alternately with sour milk to first mixture. Bake at 350° for 45 min.

Oatmeal Cake

1 c. boiling water
1 c. brown sugar
1 c. oleo
1 c. rolled oats
1 c. white sugar
2 beaten eggs

1 tsp. cinnamon
1 tsp. soda
½ tsp. salt
1 tsp. baking powder
1 tsp. vanilla
1⅓ c. flour

Pour boiling water over brown sugar, oleo and rolled oats. Sift dry ingredients. Add all together and mix well. Bake at 350° for 30 - 40 min.

Icing:

6 Tbsp. butter
½ c. brown sugar

1 c. coconut and nuts
½ c. rich milk or cream

Carrot Cake

2 c. flour
2 c. sugar
1 tsp. soda
1 tsp. salt

1 c. cooking oil
4 eggs
3 c. grated carrots
1 tsp. cinnamon

Sift dry ingredients together. Beat in oil and eggs. Stir in carrots and cinnamon. Bake in a 13" x 9" pan at 350° for 25 - 30 min.

Cream Cheese Frosting:
$\frac{1}{2}$ stick butter
4 oz. cream cheese
$\frac{1}{2}$ box confectioner's sugar

$\frac{1}{2}$ c. chopped nuts
Milk

Cream together butter, cream cheese, sugar and nuts. Add enough milk to spread easily.

Zucchini Cake

2 c. flour
2 c. sugar
1 Tbsp. cinnamon
1 tsp. salt
2 tsp. soda
1 tsp. baking powder

1 c. oil
3 eggs
2 tsp. vanilla
2 c. grated zucchini
1$\frac{1}{2}$ c. chopped nuts

In large bowl combine flour, cinnamon, baking soda, baking powder, salt, oil, vanilla and eggs. Beat at medium speed until well mixed. Stir in zucchini, raisins and 1 c. nuts. Pour into greased and floured 13" x 9" x 2" pan. Sprinkle with $\frac{1}{2}$ c. nuts. Bake at 350° for 50 min.

Cream Cheese Frosting
8 oz. softened cream cheese
2 c. 10x sugar
1 stick margarine or butter, softened

1 tsp. vanilla
$\frac{1}{4}$ c. cocoa, if desired

Cream margarine and cream cheese well. Add vanilla. Beat in sugar a little at a time.

Coffee Cake

1 box white or yellow cake mix
1 box instant vanilla pudding
1 box instant butterscotch pudding

4 eggs
1 c. vegetable oil
1 c. water

Mix all ingredients together.

Topping:
1 c. brown sugar
1 c. ground nuts

2 tsp. cinnamon

Mix together. Put half of cake batter in a 9" x 13" cake pan. Sprinkle half of topping on cake, then add rest of batter and the remaining crumbs on top of cake. Bake at 350° for 40 min. or until done.

Strawberry Short Cake

1 c. sugar
1/3 c. shortening
1 egg, separated

1/2 c. sweet milk
1 3/4 c. flour
1 tsp. baking powder

Cream sugar and shortening until smooth. Beat egg yolks with 1 tsp. milk, add and stir until well blended. Sift dry ingredients, and add with milk. Add well beaten egg white last. Bake at 350° until brown. Serve hot with cold milk and mashed strawberries.

Fruit Cake

1 1/4 c. sugar
2 eggs
1/2 c. vegetable oil
1 c. applesauce
2 c. flour

2 tsp. baking soda
1/2 tsp. salt
1 1/2 c. peaches, drained
    (any other fruit may be used)

Combine all ingredients and mix well. Bake at 350° for 30 min. Delicious in cupcakes.

Party Cupcakes

Use any good white cake recipe. Divide into portions and add a different flavor of undissolved jello to each portion. Put in cupcake pans and bake.

Jiffy Chocolate Cupcakes

1 egg
1/2 c. cocoa
1/2 c. oil
2 c. sifted cake flour
1/2 c. sour milk

1 tsp. vanilla
1 tsp. soda
1 c. sugar
1/2 tsp. salt
1/2 c. hot water

Put into mixing bowl in order given. Beat 4 min. with egg beater. Fill greased muffin tins half full. Bake at 375° for 15 - 20 min.

Favorite Frosting

3 heaping tsp. creamy peanut butter
3 heaping Tbsp. soft butter
1 tsp. vanilla

3 c. powdered sugar
1/8 tsp. salt
2 - 4 Tbsp. milk

Mix together first 3 ingredients. Stir in powdered sugar and salt. Add milk stirring to desired spreading consistency. Use your favorite layer cake or cupcakes.

"No Cook" Frosting

1/4 c. sugar
2 egg whites
1/4 tsp. salt

3/4 c. Karo
1 1/4 tsp. vanilla

Beat egg whites and salt until soft peaks form. Add sugar gradually, beating until smooth and glossy. Beat in Karo a little at a time until frosting peaks. Fold in vanilla. Makes enough for a 2 layer cake.

Karo Frosting

½ c. butter or oleo
⅓ c. Karo
2 Tbsp. milk

¼ tsp. salt
½ tsp. vanilla
1 lb. powdered sugar

Beat until smooth.

Chocolate Butter Cream Frosting

½ c. shortening
½ c. butter
1 tsp. vanilla

4 c. 10x sugar
2 Tbsp. milk
½ c. cocoa

Cream shortening and butter, then gradually beat in rest of ingredients. Add a little more milk if icing seems too thick.

How To Bake a Cake

Preheat oven; get out utensils and ingredients.
Remove blocks and toy autos from table
Grease pan, crack nuts. Measure 2 cups flour; remove baby's hands from flour, wash flour off baby.
Remeasure flour. Put flour, baking powder and salt in sifter.
Get dustpan and brush up pieces of bowl baby knocked on floor.
Get another bowl.
Answer doorbell.
Return to kitchen. Remove baby's hands from bowl.
Wash baby.
Answer phone.
Return. Remove 1/4" salt from greased pan.
Look for baby. Grease another pan.
Answer telephone.
Return to kitchen and find baby. Remove his hands from bowl.
Take up greased pan and find layer of nutshells in it.
Head for baby, who flees, knocking bowl off table.
Wash kitchen floor, tables, walls, dishes.
Call baker.

Notes

Cookies

ชิ

Which One Shall I Choose?

I face a grave decision,
  I have a choice to make,
I know I can't have both–
  So which one shall I take?

I love my little girls,
  All three are dear to me,
They're sunbeams in our home,
  Innocent and carefree.

But I also like nice flowers,
  That brighten up the sill,
I like clean floors and windows,
  Sparkling clean—but still.

I think I'll choose my babies,
  Above the pretty flowers,
Above the clean and sparkling house,
  Above the quiet hours.

I've tried it quite awhile
  I think it's long enough,
I tried to have them both,
  And it was pretty tough.

So if you stop in some day
  And the house is in a mess,
Remember I have chosen
  Which I felt was best.

For when I stand at Heaven's gate,
  Awaiting my reward,
I'm sure it would be pleasing
  To my Master and my Lord.

If I brought with me my children
  Whom I taught the best I knew,
Took time for Bible stories
  And taught them songs as they
                              grew.

Chocolate Chip Cookies

2 c. Wesson oil
4 eggs
3 c. brown sugar
2 tsp. vanilla

2 tsp. soda
2 tsp. salt
5 level c. Gold Medal flour
12 oz. chocolate chips

Mix together first four ingredients, then add soda, salt, flour and chips. Bake at 350° for 8 - 10 min. Be sure not to overbake.

Chocolate Chip Cookie Bars

1 1/2 c. soft margarine
4 1/2 c. brown sugar
6 eggs
3 tsp. vanilla
4 1/2 c. flour

4 1/2 tsp. baking powder
1 1/2 tsp. salt
2 c. chocolate chips or
    butterscotch chips
1/2 c. nuts

This makes 3 9" x 13" cake pans full. Bake at 325°. Do not overbake. Cut in squares to serve.

Brownies
(Good and Easy Bar)

1/3 c. margarine
3/4 c. sugar
1/3 c. honey
2 tsp. vanilla

1/2 c. unsifted all-purpose flour
1/2 c. cocoa
1 c. nuts

Cream margarine and sugar. Blend in honey and vanilla. Add eggs, one at a time, beating well each time. Combine flour and cocoa and gradually add to the creamed mixture. Stir in the nuts. Bake in a 9" baking dish for 25 - 30 min. at 350°.

Brownies

³/₄ c. oleo or butter
¹/₂ c. brown sugar
¹/₂ c. white sugar
3 eggs, separated
1 tsp. vanilla

2 c. flour
1 tsp. baking powder
¹/₂ tsp. salt
¹/₄ tsp. soda

Dough will be very stiff. Spread thin on shallow cake pan. Beat egg whites until frothy. Add 1 c. brown sugar and beat until stiff. Put on top. Sprinkle with nuts, chocolate chips or coconut. Bake at 350° for 35 - 40 min.

Chocolate Chip Chews

²/₃ c. oil
¹/₂ c. sugar
¹/₂ c. brown sugar
3 eggs
1 tsp. vanilla

1 tsp. salt
¹/₂ tsp. baking powder
¹/₂ tsp. soda
2¹/₂ c. flour
1 c. chocolate chips

Spread into 2 9" x 13" cake pans. Bake at 350° for 20 min. Take out of oven when they look barely done.

Toll-House Cookies with Oatmeal

1 c. shortening
³/₄ c. brown sugar
³/₄ c. white sugar
2 eggs, beaten
1 tsp. hot water
1 tsp. vanilla

1¹/₂ c. sifted flour
1 tsp. soda
1 tsp. salt
2 c. oatmeal
1 c. chopped nuts
1 pkg. Toll-house chocolate chips

Mix together shortening, sugars, eggs, water and vanilla. Sift flour, soda and salt and add to first mixture. Add oatmeal, nuts and chips. Bake at 350° for 10 - 15 min.

Butterscotch Macaroons

First Part:
2 egg whites	2 tsp. vanilla
2 Tbsp. water	4 c. flaked coconut
1 c. sugar	12 oz. butterscotch bits

Second Part:
1 c. butter or soft margarine	2 egg yolks
1 c. brown sugar	1/2 tsp. salt
3 c. sifted flour	1 tsp. soda

First Part: Beat egg whites with water until soft mounds form. Add vanilla. Stir into coconut. Chill.

Second Part: Cream butter. Add brown sugar and egg yolks. Cream well. Add salt. Add flour and soda. Form into rolls and chill. Cut 1/4" pieces off of roll and top with first part. Then put a few butterscotch bits on top. Bake at 350° for approximately 12 min.

Peanut Butter Blossoms

1 c. shortening	2 tsp. vanilla
1 1/2 c. peanut butter	2 2/3 c. unsifted flour*
2/3 c. sugar	2 tsp. baking soda
2/3 c. packed brown sugar	1 tsp. salt
2 eggs	Granulated sugar
4 Tbsp. milk	1 (8 oz.) pkg. Hershey's Kisses

Cream shortening and peanut butter. Add sugar and brown sugar. Add eggs, milk and vanilla. Beat well. Combine flour, baking soda and salt. Gradually add to creamed mixture, blending thoroughly. Shape dough into 1" balls. Roll in granulated sugar. Place on ungreased cookie sheet. Bake at 375° for 10 - 12 min. Remove from oven. Immediately place unwrapped Kiss on top of each cookie, pressing down so that the cookie cracks around the edge. Remove from cookie sheet. Cool. Makes about 4 dozen cookies.

*Gold Medal flour is especially good for these cookies.

Monster Cookies

12 eggs
4 c. white sugar
4 c. brown sugar
$^1/_3$ c. vanilla
8 tsp. soda
1 lb. M & M's

2 c. nuts
1 lb. butter (do not substitute)
3 lb. peanut butter
18 c. oatmeal
1 lb. chocolate chips

Mix in order given. Bake at 350°.

Coconut Oatmeal Cookies

1$^1/_2$ c. unsifted flour
1 tsp. soda
1 tsp. salt
1 c. butter
1 c. brown sugar, firmly packed

1 c. white sugar
2 eggs
3 c. oatmeal
$^1/_2$ c. pecans, chopped
1$^1/_2$ c. Bakers coconut, grated

Mix shortening and sugar. Add eggs and mix well. Add rest of ingredients with pecans and coconut added last. Bake at 350°.

Famous Oatmeal Cookies

$^3/_4$ c. shortening
1 c. brown sugar
$^1/_2$ c. granulated sugar
1 egg
$^1/_4$ c. water

1 tsp. vanilla
1 tsp. salt
$^1/_2$ tsp. soda
1$^1/_2$ c. flour
3 c. oatmeal

Mix all ingredients and bake at 350° until almost done. They stay softer if they're not overbaked.

Oatmeal Whoopie Pies

2 c. brown sugar
³/₄ c. butter
2 eggs
¹/₂ tsp. salt
2 c. flour

2 c. oatmeal
1 tsp. cinnamon
1 tsp. baking powder
2 tsp. soda, in 3 Tbsp.
   boiling water

Combine all ingredients. Add soda and water last. Fill with your favorite filling. Bake at 350°.

Lantza's Favorite Whoopie Pies

2 c. sugar
1 c. oil
2 eggs
1 c. thick sour milk
   (add 2 tsp. soda to sour the milk)
1 c. cold water mixed with 1 tsp. instant coffee

4 c. bread flour
¹/₂ tsp. salt
1 c. cocoa
2 tsp. vanilla

Cream together sugar, salt, oil, cocoa, eggs and vanilla. Then add sour milk and cold coffee mixtures gradually with the flour. Beat well. Bake at 350°.

Filling:
   2 egg whites
   2 tsp. vanilla
   4 Tbsp. flour
   2 Tbsp. milk

1¹/₂ c. shortening
2 c. 10x sugar
1 c. marshmallow creme, optional

Beat egg whites until very stiff, then add vanilla, flour and milk and beat well. Add shortening, sugar and marshmallow creme.

Whoopie Pie Filling

2 egg whites
1 c. Crisco (scant)
2 tsp. vanilla

3 Tbsp. milk
¹/₂ c. flour, sifted
10x confectioner's sugar

Beat egg whites till stiff. Add Crisco and vanilla. Blend. Add milk then add flour and 10x sugar until smooth and thick.

Pumpkin Whoopies

2 c. pumpkin
2 egg yolks
2 c. brown sugar
1 c. vegetable oil
1 tsp. cloves
1 tsp. ginger

1 tsp. salt
1 tsp. baking powder
1 tsp. soda
1 tsp. vanilla
3 c. flour

Filling:
2 egg whites
2 tsp. vanilla
4 Tbsp. flour

$1\frac{1}{2}$ c. vegetable shortening
2 Tbsp. milk
1 lb. 10x sugar

Mix together pumpkin, egg yolks, brown sugar, vegetable oil and vanilla until creamy. Sift and add dry ingredients. Bake at 375°.

Pumpkin Cookies

1 c. oil
1 c. pumpkin
1 c. brown sugar
2 c. flour
1 tsp. soda

1 tsp. baking powder
1 egg
$\frac{1}{2}$ tsp. salt
1 tsp. cinnamon

Mix oil, pumpkin, and sugar. Add egg then rest of ingredients.

Icing:
$\frac{1}{2}$ c. brown sugar
3 Tbsp. butter
$\frac{1}{4}$ c. milk

2 c. 10x sugar
1 tsp. vanilla

Boil first 3 ingredients for 2 min. Then add sugar and vanilla.

Spicy Cookies

2 c. brown sugar
1 c. shortening
1 c. + 4 Tbsp. milk
3 eggs, beaten
2 tsp. baking powder
2 tsp. soda

1 tsp. cinnamon
1/4 tsp. cloves
1 tsp. vanilla
4 c. flour
1 c. chopped nuts

Mix in order given. Drop by teaspoon on greased cookie sheet, and bake at 375° for 10 min. Ice while warm.

Icing:
6 Tbsp. butter
3 Tbsp. hot water

1 tsp. vanilla
Powdered sugar

Brown butter. Add hot water and vanilla. Add powdered sugar until thick enough to spread.

Date Filled Cookies

Filling:
1/4 c. sugar
1/4 c. pitted dates

3/4 c. water
3/8 tsp. vanilla

Cook sugar, dates and water together until thickened then add vanilla.

Dough:
1/8 c. butter
1 1/2 c. sifted flour
1 1/2 c. quick oatmeal
1 c. brown sugar

1 tsp. soda
2 tsp. baking powder
4 Tbsp. milk

Mix like pie dough and wet with milk. Cut with round cookie cutter. Place teaspoon of filling on one disk and top with another. Bake on ungreased cookie sheet about 15 min. at 375°. These can be rolled up as a jelly roll and chilled then cut in 1/4" slices and baked.

Filled Raisin Cookies

Filling:
4 c. chopped raisins	2 c. water
4 Tbsp. flour	2 c. sugar

Boil till thick.

Dough:
2 c. sugar	2 tsp. soda
1 c. sweet milk	2 tsp. baking powder
4 tsp. cream of tartar	2 eggs
1 c. shortening	2 tsp. vanilla
7 c. flour	

Roll out the dough, cut with round cutter. Put 1 tsp. filling on cookie. Make another cookie slightly larger to put on top. Make a little hole in center so filling stays in cookie. Do not press together. Bake at 350° approximately 13 min.

Soft Molasses Cookies

1 c. oil	1 tsp. ginger
2 c. brown sugar	$1/2$ tsp. salt
1 c. Brer Rabbit molasses	3 tsp. soda
2 c. sour milk	2 tsp. cinnamon
2 eggs	6 c. flour
1 tsp. vanilla	

Mix in order given. Bake at 400°.

Icing:
3 c. 10x sugar	2 Tbsp. soft butter

Add just enough water to make a soft icing. Spread on cookies when they are cool.

Good Walnut Cookies

2 c. brown sugar
1 c. butter
1 c. chopped nuts
2 eggs

2 tsp. soda
1 tsp. cream of tartar
Pinch of salt
3½ c. flour

Shape into rolls. Let set overnight. Slice and bake.

Crescents
(Christmas Treats)

½ c. 10x sugar
½ lb. butter
¼ tsp. salt

1¾ c. flour
1 c. chopped nuts
1 tsp. vanilla

Cream butter and sugar. Add salt, flour and vanilla then add nuts. Roll into balls or crescent shapes and bake at 350° for 10 min. Roll in 10x sugar.

Aunt Sadie's Sand Tarts

3 sticks butter
2½ c. granulated sugar
4 eggs
2 tsp. vanilla

1 tsp. salt
6 c. flour
4 tsp. baking powder

Roll out thin and cut into decorative shapes. Sprinkle with your favorite decorations or egg whites and cinnamon and nuts. Bake at 350° a very short time.

Cream Puffs

½ c. butter
1 c. boiling water
1 c. flour, sifted

¼ tsp. salt
4 eggs, unbeaten

In a saucepan, bring shortening and water to a boil. Sift flour and salt together; add to water all at once and beat vigorously until mixture is thick and smooth and comes away from sides of pan easily. Remove from heat and add eggs, one at a time, beating well after each addition until mixture is smooth and blended. Drop from tablespoon about 2" apart onto greased baking sheet. (Mixture should hold its shape and not spread.) Bake at 450° for 10 min.; reduce heat to 400° and bake 25 min. longer. Cool; slit each puff and fill with cream filling. Dust with confectioner's sugar. Yield: 18.

Cream filling:
1 c. sugar
⅔ c. flour
Dash of salt

4 c. milk
4 egg yolks, slightly beaten
2 tsp. vanilla

Mix sugar, flour and salt together thoroughly; add milk and mix well. Add egg yolks and blend. Place over hot water in double boiler and cook until smooth and thick, stirring constantly. (About 2 min.) Cool, stirring occasionally to prevent a skin forming on top. Makes enough filling for 18 puffs.

Icing:
1 c. shortening
½ c. butter
½ c. peanut butter

Add enough 10x sugar to make a soft icing.

There's one sad truth in life I've found while journeying east to west.
The only folks we really wound are those we love the best.
We flatter those we scarcely know,
we please the fleeting guest and
deal full many a thoughtless blow to those who love us best.

❧ Notes ❧

Pies

ટ

Sunshine Pie

A pound of patience you must find
Mixed well with loving words so kind.
Drop in two pounds of helpful deeds
And thoughts of other people's needs.

A pack of smiles, to make the crust,
Then stir and bake it well you must.
And now, I ask that you may try,
The recipe of this Sunshine Pie.

ટ

Recipe for Better Understanding

1 cupful of listening when the person speaks; measure words carefully. Add a heaping teaspoonful of sympathetic consideration. Sift together to get a smooth batter for a consistent reply. Use generous amounts of longsuffering and forbearing, tempered with mercy. Cook on front burners; keep temperature low and do not boil. Add a pinch of warm personality and clear unhurried speech. Season to taste, using possibly a dash of humor to bring out a good flavor.
Serve in individual molds.

Strawberry Pie

2 c. crushed strawberries
3 Tbsp. strawberry jello
3 Tbsp. cornstarch

1 c. water
1 c. sugar

Mix and cook for 2 min. When this mixture is partly cool, add 2 c. fresh cut up strawberries. Put into baked pie crust and top with whipped cream. Cool 2 hrs.

Strawberry Pie

$\frac{1}{2}$ c. sugar
$\frac{1}{2}$ pt. whipping cream
1 tsp. vanilla
3 oz. cream cheese

1$\frac{1}{2}$ qt. strawberries
$\frac{1}{2}$ c. sugar
1$\frac{1}{2}$ Tbsp. cornstarch

Blend together cream cheese, vanilla and $\frac{1}{2}$ c. sugar. Fold in whipped cream and pour mixture into baked and chilled pie crust. Cook together 1$\frac{1}{2}$ Tbsp. cornstarch and 1 pt. strawberry juice (mashed and strained). Stir and cook this mixture until thick and clear, boil about 5 min. On top place 1 qt. of berries and pour cooled mixture over top. Makes 1 9" pie.

Fresh Peach Pie

1$\frac{1}{2}$ c. water
$\frac{1}{4}$ c. clear jell

1$\frac{1}{2}$ c. sugar
3 Tbsp. orange jello

Boil water, sugar and clear jell together. Then add jello and cool. Slice plenty of peaches and add just enough of this mixture to hold them together. Pour into baked pie crust or graham cracker crust and top with whipped topping. Chill at least 2 hrs. before serving. This mixture should make 3 8" pies if you use enough peaches. Top with whipped topping.

French Rhubarb Pie

1 egg
1 c. sugar
1 tsp. vanilla

2 c. diced rhubarb
1 Tbsp. flour

Mix all together. Put mixture into unbaked pie shell.

Topping:
3/4 c. flour
1/2 c. brown sugar

1/3 c. butter

Melt butter and mix with flour and sugar and pour over rhubarb mixture. Bake at 400° for 10 min. Continue baking at 350° for 35 min.

Church Apple Pie Filling

2 heaping c. apples, sliced roughly
Water to cover apples
1 c. granulated sugar

1/4 tsp. salt
1 c. water
2 Tbsp. clear jell

Mix all ingredients and cook till thick. Cool and use as pie filling.

Delicious Quick Apple Pie Filling

1 gal. sliced apples, syrup packed
1 gal. water
6 c. granulated sugar

1/4 c. lemon juice
1/2 tsp. salt
Thicken with clear jell

Cinnamon or nutmeg may be added. Makes 15 8" pies.

If your day is hemmed with prayer,
it is less likely to unravel. ➢

Can Apple Pie Filling

4½ c. sugar
1 c. cornstarch
½ tsp. salt
2 tsp. cinnamon
¼ tsp. nutmeg

10 c. water
3 Tbsp. lemon juice
3 drops yellow food coloring
16 c. sliced uncooked apples

Cook all ingredients together except for apples. Add them then cold pack for 25 min. This mixture may set in the jars. It will make nice pies anyway.

Fruit Pie Filling

Pit and wash and cut up fruit if necessary. Put fruit in a pan and cover with water. Add just enough sugar to suit your taste. Bring to a boil and add a thickener like clear jell or tapioca. Chill the filling then put between two pie crusts and bake for 45 min. at 350°.

Good N' Plenty Pecan Pie

½ c. sugar
1 c. light corn syrup
4 Tbsp. butter

3 eggs
1 tsp. vanilla
½ c. whole or chopped pecans

Boil sugar, syrup and butter together. Beat eggs and fold into syrup. Add vanilla and pecans. Bake at 350° for 30 min. Makes 1 pie.

Boi

Custard Pie

4 eggs, separated
¾ c. white sugar
Dash of salt

1 tsp. vanilla
2⅔ c. milk (bring to boiling)

Mix this together, then beat the egg whites stiff and add to yolk mixture. Bake at 450° for 15 min. then at 350° until done. Use only 3 eggs for an 8" pan.

Raisin Custard Pie

2 c. raisins
2 c. sugar
2 c. water
1 tsp. salt

4 Tbsp. flour
2 eggs
1 tsp. vinegar

Stew raisins until soft, add flour, sugar, egg yolks, water, vinegar, and salt. Let come to a boil and keep stirring. Cool and pour into baked crust. Top with Cool Whip.

Coconut Custard Pie

4 eggs, slightly beaten
½ tsp. salt
1 tsp. vanilla

⅔ c. sugar
2⅔ c. milk, scalded
1 c. coconut

Add sugar and salt to beaten eggs. Add milk and vanilla. Stir in coconut. Pour in unbaked pie shell and bake for 25 min. in a 425° oven. Put pan of water on bottom of oven rack while baking pie. Top with Cool Whip when cold.

Coconut Cream Pie

1/2 c. sugar
1/2 tsp. salt
3 Tbsp. cornstarch
2 1/2 c. milk

3 egg yolks, beaten
1 Tbsp. butter
1 tsp. vanilla
1/2 c. coconut, fine

Cook all this together. When cooled off add some Cool Whip and put in baked pie crusts. Put Cool Whip on top and garnish with a little coconut.

Boston Cream Pie

4 egg yolks
9 Tbsp. water
1 1/2 c. sugar

2 c. flour
3 tsp. baking powder
1/2 tsp. salt

Chocolate Glaze:
  2 Tbsp. butter
  1 sq. unsweetened chocolate or
    1 Tbsp. cocoa

2 Tbsp. boiling water
1 c. 10x sugar

Beat egg yolks. Add water, beating well. Add sugar slowly, beating all the while. Sift the flour. Put in baking powder and salt. Add to first mixture. Beat well. Beat egg whites until stiff and fold into batter. Pour in cake pan. Bake at 350° for 30 - 35 min.

Creme Filling:
  1/2 c. sugar
  1/4 c. cornstarch
  1/4 tsp. salt

2 c. milk
4 egg yolks
1/2 tsp. vanilla

Heat milk. Mix sugar, egg yolks, cornstarch and salt. Slowly add to milk and stir until thick.

Vanilla Pie

2 c. brown sugar
2 heaping Tbsp. flour
2 c. molasses, scant
2 heaping Tbsp. clear jell

2 tsp. vanilla
4 eggs
1 qt. water

Crumbs:
  2 c. flour
  $^3/_4$ c. brown sugar
  $^1/_4$ c. lard

  $^1/_2$ tsp. soda
  $^1/_2$ tsp. cream of tartar

Mix brown sugar and flour. Add molasses, water and vanilla. Heat, then add beaten eggs. Then add clear jell mixed with $^1/_2$ c. water. Stir until thick. Pour into 3 8" pie crusts. Cover with crumbs. Bake at 425° for 10 min., then at 350° for 30 min.

Butterscotch Pie

2 c. brown sugar
$^1/_2$ c. hot water
2 Tbsp. butter

3 heaping Tbsp. flour
2 eggs
$2^1/_2$ c. milk

Boil sugar, water and butter together until it scorches. Make a custard with flour, eggs and milk and add to first mixture, stirring constantly. Put into baked pie crust then top with Cool Whip.

Peanut Butter Pie

1 9" graham cracker crust
1 lg. pkg. instant vanilla pudding
1 c. 10x sugar

$^1/_2$ c. peanut butter
1 pkg. Cool Whip (medium)

Mix sugar and peanut butter; spread some on bottom of pie crust. Mix pudding as directed, but use only $1^1/_2$ c. milk. When pudding is partially set fold in Cool Whip and pour over crust. Top with Cool Whip and the rest of the crumbs.

Peanut Butter Pie

4 oz. cream cheese
1/2 c. milk
1/3 c. 10x sugar

1/3 c. peanut butter
Cool Whip

Mix all ingredients well with beater. Fold in about 3/4 box (8 oz. box) Cool Whip. Pour into 8" graham cracker crust. Freeze or chill.

Peanut Butter Pie

1 9" baked pie shell
1/3 c. peanut butter
3/4 c. powdered sugar
1/3 c. flour
1/2 c. sugar

1/8 tsp. salt
2 c. milk, scalded
3 egg yolks, beaten
2 Tbsp. butter
1 tsp. vanilla

Blend peanut butter and powdered sugar until mealy. Spread 2/3 of this mixture over pie shell. Reserve remainder. Combine flour, sugar and salt in double boiler. Stir in egg yolks; cook a few minutes. Add vanilla and butter; mix well, then cool.

Meringue:
3 egg whites
1/4 tsp. cream of tartar

1/2 c. sugar
1 tsp. cornstarch

Beat egg whites until foamy. Add cream of tartar, sugar, and cornstarch mixture, a little at a time, beating until stiff. Cover pie with meringue. Sprinkle remaining peanut butter and sugar mixture over top of meringue. Bake 12 - 15 min. at 350°. Cool, then chill in refrigerator.

Lemon Sponge Pie

2 c. granulated sugar
1 grated lemon (1/3 c. juice)
2 Tbsp. melted butter

4 Tbsp. flour, rounded
4 eggs, separated
2 1/2 c. milk

Mix sugar and flour. Add melted butter, lemon, milk and beaten egg yolks. Add egg whites (beaten stiff) last. Bake at 350° for approximately 40 min.

Lemon Meringue Pie

1 egg
2 c. sugar
4 Tbsp. flour, rounded

1 qt. water
1/4 c. butter
1/2 c. Real Lemon

Mix together and pour into a 9" pie shell. Top with meringue.

Meringue:
4 egg whites
1/2 tsp. salt

1 tsp. cream of tartar
1 c. sugar

Beat egg whites, salt and cream of tartar until foamy. Add sugar, 1 Tbsp. at a time. Beat for 10 min. Place pies in a 425° oven for 5 min. (until brown on top).

Grandma's Favorite Pumpkin Pie

1 1/2 c. pumpkin
3/4 c. granulated sugar
3 eggs
1 tsp. vanilla

3/4 c. brown sugar
1/4 c. flour
2 c. milk
2 Tbsp. browned butter

Measure pumpkin, brown sugar, granulated sugar, egg yolks and flour into bowl and beat very well. Then add 2 c. scalded milk, vanilla and brown butter. Beat egg whites and fold in last. Fill your pie crusts to the brim and sprinkle with cinnamon. Bake at 425° for 15 min., then 325° for 30 min.

Ice Cream Pumpkin Pie

1 1/2 c. cooked pumpkin
1/2 c. brown sugar
1/2 tsp. salt
1 tsp. cinnamon
1/4 tsp. ginger

1/8 tsp. cloves
1 qt. softened vanilla ice cream
1 lg. graham cracker crust
Whipped cream

Combine pumpkin with brown sugar and spices. Fold into ice cream. Pour into crust. Cover and freeze until firm. Serve with whipped cream.

Rice Krispie Ice Cream Pie

1/4 c. butter   5 c. Rice Krispies
1/2 lb. marshmallows

Melt butter and marshmallows. Turn burner off and add Rice Krispies. Put in pie plate and put ice cream on top.

Wet Bottom Shoofly

Liquid: Crumbs:
  3 c. molasses   6 c. flour
  3 c. hot water   2 c. brown sugar
  2 tsp. soda   1 c. lard
  1 c. brown sugar   1 tsp. soda
  6 eggs, beaten

Makes 4 pies or 1 cake (9" x 13"). Put half of crumbs to liquid and half on top. Bake at 425° for 10 min. then at 350° for 40 min.

Shoo-Fly Pie

2 c. molasses   1/3 c. brown sugar
2 tsp. baking soda   2 1/4 c. boiling water

Mix together, then let cool.

Crumbs:
  3 c. regular flour   1 c. lard
  2 c. whole wheat flour   2 c. brown sugar
  1 tsp. soda

Beat 2 eggs in molasses mixture, then add 3 1/2 c. crumb mixture. Put into pie crusts, then sprinkle the rest of crumbs on top. Bake at 400° for 20 min., then at 375° for 25 min.

Gooey Shoo-Fly Pie

Liquid:
- 6 eggs, beaten
- 1 c. granulated sugar
- 1 c. brown sugar
- 5 c. molasses (golden)
- 6 c. boiling water
- 2 tsp. baking soda (heaping)

Crumbs:
- 3 lb. regular flour
- $1\frac{1}{2}$ lb. bread flour
- $2\frac{3}{4}$ lb. brown sugar
- $1\frac{1}{4}$ lb. lard
- 1 tsp. baking soda

Mix liquid ingredients together and set aside. Mix crumb mixture all together until thoroughly mixed. Add 11 c. of crumbs to liquid mixture and mix well. Pour into 10 unbaked pie crusts. Bake for 1 hr. at 350°.

Chocolate Shoo Fly Pies

- 2 c. brown sugar
- 1 c. shortening
- 2 eggs
- 4 Tbsp. cocoa
- 2 c. molasses
- 2 tsp. soda

- 2 c. hot water
- 2 tsp. vanilla
- $\frac{1}{2}$ tsp. cinnamon
- $\frac{1}{4}$ tsp. salt
- $4\frac{1}{2}$ - 5 c. flour

Cream together brown sugar and shortening. Add eggs and cocoa. Soak together molasses, soda and hot water then add to first mixture. Add rest of ingredients.

Chocolate Pudding for Shoo Fly Pies:
- 2 c. sugar
- 2 Tbsp. flour
- 2 Tbsp. butter
- 2 eggs

- 2 Tbsp. cornstarch
- 3 Tbsp. cocoa
- 2 c. water
- 1 tsp. vanilla

Boil ingredients together. Cool pudding, then put in unbaked pie shell. Then put the chocolate mix on next and bake at 350° for 45 - 50 min. When pies are cool, top with your favorite icing. This should make approx. 8 8" pies.

Snitz Pies

10 lb. dried apples
4 lemons, sliced

20 c. sugar (more if desired)
3 level Tbsp. cinnamon

Soak apples overnight in water, use 2c. of the water to cook them. You may need more. Stir, when soft put through press, add sugar and cinnamon. If the mixture seems a little thin add some clear jell or minute tapioca. Makes 40 church pies.

Snitz Pie

1 gal. apple butter
6 qt. applesauce
14 c. sugar (7 brown & 7 white)
1 tsp. salt

2 tsp. cinnamon
$^3/_4$ tsp. nutmeg
2 c. clear jell or flour

Mix clear jell and sugar, then add enough water to make it thin. Add to rest of ingredients. Pour into unbaked pie shells and put a dough top on. Make a hole in center of dough. Brush top of pies with well beaten eggs, then sprinkle with crumbs. Bake at 350° for 1 hr. Makes 22 8" pies.

Crumbs:
1 c. flour
$^1/_4$ c. lard

$^1/_2$ c. brown sugar

Mix until fine.

Dependable Pie Crust

4$^1/_2$ lb. flour
2 lb. lard
$^1/_2$ c. cornstarch

$^1/_2$ Tbsp. baking powder
1 c. 10x sugar
$^1/_2$ Tbsp. salt

Mix into a crumb consistency. Add enough water to be able to roll it out. Depending on the lard you may need a few more cups of flour. Crisco may be used instead of lard, it is a bit more dependable.

Breads and Rolls

ﻬ

Friends

When good friends walk beside us,
On the trials that we must keep
Our burdens seem less heavy
And the hills are not so steep
The weary miles pass swiftly
Taken in a joyous stride
And all the world seems brighter
When friends walk by thy side.

ﻬ

Recipe for Life

1 c. good thoughts
3 c. forgiveness
1 c. kind deeds

2 c. well-beaten faults
1 c. consideration for others

Mix thoroughly and add tears of joy, sorrow and sympathy for others. Fold in 4 c. of prayer and faith to lighten other ingredients and raise the texture to great heights of Christian living. After pouring all this into your daily life, bake well with the warmth of human kindness. Serve with a smile.

Bread

2 Tbsp. yeast, in 1 c. warm water
2 Tbsp. sugar
4 Tbsp. Karo
4 Tbsp. Wesson oil

½ Tbsp. sugar
Pinch of salt
2 c. hot water
8 - 9 c. bread flour

Add sugar to the yeast and warm water. Let stand until it foams. Mix the Karo, oil, sugar, pinch of salt and hot water. Mix yeast mixture and add flour. Mix all together and let rise until double. Punch down. Let rise again, then shape in 1 lb. loaves. Let rise until double. Bake at 350° for 25 - 30 min. Butter the warm loaves of bread and cool before putting in bags.

Bread

2 Tbsp. yeast in 1 c. water and
1 tsp. sugar
¾ c. oil

½ c. sugar
1 Tbsp. salt
4 c. lukewarm water

Dissolve the yeast in the water and sugar. Put the oil, ½ c. sugar, salt and rest of water in a bowl. Last add yeast mixture. Put in flour until somewhat sticky, beating well. Let rise. Punch down when doubled in size. Let rise again until double. Then knead well and put into loaf pans. Let rise till double. Bake at 375° for 30 min.

Whole Wheat Bread

5 c. whole wheat flour
13 - 14 c. white flour
1 c. sugar
1 c. melted lard

3 pkgs. yeast dissolved in
  1 c. warm water
2 Tbsp. salt
6 c. hot water

Mix sugar, salt, shortening, water, whole wheat flour, and about 4 c. white flour. Add dissolved yeast. Add remaining flour and knead about 10 min. Let rise for 2 - 3 hrs. Knead and let rise again. Bake bread at 350° for 30 min. Yield: 5 or 6 loaves.

100% Whole Wheat Bread

1 1/2 qt. warm water
2 Tbsp. yeast
4 tsp. salt
3 tsp. vinegar
10 c. whole wheat flour

3 tsp. lecithin
3 tsp. Blackstrap molasses
4 eggs
2/3 c. safflower oil

Put 1 qt. warm water in large bowl. Add yeast; set aside. Now get all the other ingredients ready. In a 2 c. measure, put oil; now mix in lecithin and blackstrap. Beat the eggs. By now, the yeast mixture is ready for more ingredients. Add salt, vinegar and oil mixture, also eggs. Fill a quart can half full with warm water, put in honey to 3/4, stir well and add to mixture. Now add 10 c. of whole wheat flour; stir well. Add 8 more, a little at a time. Knead well. Knead every 15 min. for 2 1/2 hrs. Put in pans and bake at 350° or 400° for 30 min. When baked butter well and put in bags. Good luck. Makes 6 loaves.

Sister Mary's Whole Wheat Bread

1 Tbsp. yeast (rounded) in 1/2 c. lukewarm water and 1 tsp. sugar
1/3 c. sugar or honey
3 c. hot water
1 Tbsp. salt
1/2 c. oil

5 c. whole wheat flour
2 c. occident flour

Mix sugar, hot water and salt. Add flour. If you can't get the occident flour, just use your favorite white bread flour.

Zucchini Bread

3 eggs
2 c. sugar
1 c. oil
2 c. grated peeled zucchini
3 c. flour
1 tsp. grated lemon rind, optional

2 tsp. cinnamon
1 tsp. baking powder
1 tsp. baking soda
1 tsp. salt
1 c. chopped nuts, optional

Beat eggs until light and fluffy. Add sugar, oil, and vanilla, mixing until thick. Add zucchini, stir thoroughly. Sift dry ingredients. Add, stirring until smooth. Bake 1 hr. in 350° oven in 2 floured loaf pans.

Pumpkin Bread

2 c. pumpkin
1 c. salad oil
3 c. sugar
4 beaten eggs
3¼ c. flour
1 tsp. baking powder

1 tsp. baking soda
1 tsp. ground cloves
1 tsp. nutmeg
1 tsp. cinnamon
1 tsp. salt
1 c. walnuts, chopped

Mix all ingredients together. Pour into greased and floured bread pans. Bake at 350° for 1 hr. Makes 3 small loaves.

Banana Bread

2 eggs
½ c. shortening
3 bananas, mashed
1 tsp. soda

Pinch of salt
1 c. sugar
2 c. flour

Mix together in order given. Bake in bread pan 350° until done.

Raisin Bread

15 oz. raisins
1 c. warm water
½ c. oil
1 Tbsp. cinnamon
2 eggs, beaten

2 Tbsp. dry yeast
2 c. warm milk
½ c. sugar
1 Tbsp. salt
8 - 10 c. flour

Soak raisins 3 - 4 hrs. or overnight. Drain. Dissolve yeast in warm water. Combine milk, oil, sugar, cinnamon, salt and eggs. Beat well. Add yeast and raisins. Gradually add flour, stirring by hand. When dough becomes too stiff to beat finish working in flour with hands. Place dough in greased bowl. Cover and let rise in warm place about 1 hr. Punch down, knead and let rise another hour. Divide dough into 5 portions and form loaves. Place in greased pans and let rise another hour. Bake at 350° for 50 - 60 min.

Icing:
1 c. 10x sugar
1 tsp. vanilla

1 Tbsp. soft butter

Mix well and add enough water to easily spread over bread.

Bubble Bread

1 c. milk, scalded
1/2 c. sugar
1 tsp. salt
2 Tbsp. yeast
2 beaten eggs

4 1/2 c. flour
1 stick butter
1 c. sugar
1 Tbsp. cinnamon
1/2 c. nuts

Mix sugar and salt with milk and cool to lukewarm. Add yeast and eggs, then flour. Knead till smooth and elastic, not sticky. Place in greased bowl and cover with damp cloth and let rise for 10 min. Meanwhile, melt butter in small pan. Mix together sugar, cinnamon and nuts. Make balls of dough size of walnut, roll each in melted butter then in sugar mixture. Place in greased angel food cake pan in taggered rows until all dough is used. Let rise and bake in 350° oven for about 40 - 45 min.

Feather Light Dinner Rolls

2 Tbsp. white sugar
1 tsp. salt
1 c. scalded milk
2 Tbsp. butter

1 egg, beaten
1/4 c. water
1 c. flour
1 Tbsp. yeast

Pour scalded milk over salt and sugar. Melt butter in hot milk. Let cool to lukewarm. Add rest of ingredients. Let this get bubbly, then add 3 c. bread flour. Let rise, then work down and let rise again, then make dinner rolls or put in cup cake pans. 1/2 c. whole wheat flour may be used if desired. Bake at 350° until browned.

Aunt Edna's Delicious Rolls

1 Tbsp. dry yeast
³/₄ c. lukewarm water
1 Tbsp. sugar
1 c. scalded milk

2 tsp. salt
3 Tbsp. sugar
4 Tbsp. shortening
1 well beaten egg

Put together yeast, warm water and 1 Tbsp. sugar. Let stand 10 min. Put salt, 3 Tbsp. sugar and shortening in scalded milk. When milk is warm add to yeast mixture and eggs. Add flour and knead into soft elastic dough (a softer dough than for bread). Let rise in warm place until double in size. Fold down and let rise again. Roll dough out and spread with butter. Sprinkle with brown sugar and cinnamon. Put together like jelly roll. Cut with knife about 1" thick. Let rise in greased pan till double. Bake at 400° for 15 - 20 min. When cooled put on your favorite icing. These are also delicious when used for church rolls.

Soft Pretzels

4 tsp. yeast
¹/₂ tsp. salt
2 Tbsp. brown sugar

1¹/₂ c. warm water
1 Tbsp. oil

Add approximately 4¹/₂ c. flour. Knead like you would bread dough. Let rise till double and then roll into pretzels any size you wish. Dip pretzels into a mixture of 2 tsp. soda and 1 c. warm water. Sprinkle with coarse salt. Then bake in a very hot oven at 500° just until they are brown, approx. 10 min. When you get them out of the oven dip them in melted butter. Delicious with a glass of ice cold lemonade.

Stromboli

Dough:
   1¹/₃ c. warm water
   2 Tbsp. oil

1 Tbsp. yeast
¹/₂ tsp. salt

Add 4 - 5 c. flour and knead well. Let rise till double. Then knead again and divide dough into 3 pieces. Roll out dough to approximately ¹/₄" thick. Layer with slices of chopped ham and cheese, (or whatever you prefer). Fold up edges and pinch together. Spread a generous amount of butter on top and sprinkle with seasoning salt. Bake at 350° for 25 min. Let set 15 min. then cut and serve.

Doughnuts

2 tsp. sugar, dissolved in
1/2 c. warm water
1 yeast cake
1 c. scalded milk
2 tsp. salt
1 c. sugar

2 1/4 c. flour, sifted
4 eggs
1 c. hot mashed potatoes
1 c. melted shortening
5 c. flour or more

Add yeast to the sugar and water mixture in a large bowl. Combine the scalded milk, salt and sugar. Let it cool, then add yeast solution to milk solution. Blend in 2 1/4 c. flour, sifted. Let it stand 1 hr., then add eggs, potatoes and shortening. Add 5 c. of flour or more. Mix well, then raise again. Roll and cut them. Put in warm place to rise again. Fry in deep fat.

Pizza Dough

1 pkg. dry yeast
1 1/2 tsp. salt
1/2 c. shortening
5 c. flour

2 Tbsp. water
2 1/2 tsp. sugar
2 c. boiling water

Put yeast, 2 Tbsp. water and sugar into bowl. Set aside. Put 2 c. boiling water in bowl. Add shortening and salt. Stir in 2 c. flour with wire whip or electric beater. When mixture is just warm, beat in yeast mix. Stir in rest of flour. Let rest for 5 - 10 min. Pat into pizza pan and proceed with toppings.

Egg Noodles

3 egg yolks
1 whole egg

3 Tbsp. cold water
2 c. flour (approximately)

Beat eggs slightly, add cold water, add flour to make a stiff dough. Turn out on floured board, knead 3 - 5 min. Divide into 3 parts and roll each into a paper thin sheet. Place on large cloth on a table to dry slightly about 1 hr. Then roll up dough like jelly roll, cut crosswise about 1/8" strips or desired thickness. Spread cut noodles loosely on table to dry thoroughly. Makes 6 c. noodles.

The Many Uses of Stale Bread

Take a half dozen slices of stale bread of equal size and place in a hot oven a few minutes to become crisped on the outside so they may be quickly toasted over a hot fire, a delicate brown. Butter them and for breakfast serve with a poached egg on each slice.

A plate of hot, crisp, nicely-browned and buttered toast is always a welcome addition to the breakfast table.

Serve creamed asparagus tips on slices of toast for luncheon.

The economical housewife carefully inspects the contents of her bread box and refrigerator every morning before planning her meals for the day, and is particular to use scraps of bread and left-over meat and vegetables as quickly as possible. Especially is this necessary in hot weather. Never use any food unless perfectly sweet and fresh. If otherwise, it is unfit for use.

Loaves of bread which have become stale can be freshened if wrapped in a damp cloth for a few minutes, then removed and placed in a hot oven until heated through.

For a change, toast slices of stale bread quite crisp and serve a plate of hot, plain toast at a table, to be easten broken in small pieces in individual bowls of milk. Still another way is to put the stiffly-beaten white of an egg on the center of a hot, buttered slice of taost, carefully drop the yolk in the center of the beaten white and place in hot oven a few minutes to cook. Serve with a bit of butter on top, season with pepper and salt. Serve at once.

Another way to use stale bread is to toast slices of bread, spread with butter, pour 1 c. of hot milk over it, in which has been beaten 1 egg and a pinch of salt. Serve in a deep dish. Or a cup of hot milk may be poured over crisply-toasted sliced of buttered bread, without the addition of an egg.

ঽ৶

Mother's Musings

O, give me patience when wee hands
Tug at me with their small demands
And give me gentle and smiling eyes.
Keep my lips from hasty replies
And let not weariness, confusion or noise
Obscure my vision of life's fleeting joys.
So when in years to come my house is still
No bitter memories its rooms may fill.

Desserts

No Time

I knelt to pray, but not for long,
I had too much to do,
Must hurry off and get to work,
For bills would soon be due.

And so I said a hurried prayer,
Jumped up from off my knees;
My Christian duty now was done,
My soul could be at ease.

All through the day I had not time
To speak a word of cheer,
No time to speak of Christ to friends
They'd laugh at me, I feared.

No time, no time, too much to do—
That was my constant cry:
No time to give to those in need—
At last t'was time to die.

And when before the Lord I came,
I stood with downcast eyes,
Within His hand He held a book.
It was the "Book of Life."

God looked into His Book and said,
"Your name I cannot find,
I once was going to write it down,
But never found the time."

Peach Cobbler

6 - 8 large ripe peaches, sliced
1 c. sugar

2½ Tbsp. cornstarch

Crust:
  1 c. flour
  2 egg yolks
  ¼ c. melted butter or oleo

2 egg whites, stiffly beaten
1 tsp. baking powder
1 c. sugar

Combine peaches, cornstarch and sugar. Pour into a greased 13" x 9" x 2" pan. Combine all crust ingredients except egg whites. In separate bowl, beat egg whites until stiff. Fold egg whites into other mixture. Spread over peaches. Bake at 375° for 45 min.

Rhubarb Dessert

1½ c. sugar
2 Tbsp. clear jell

½ c. water
4 c. diced rhubarb

Crumbs:
  1 c. brown sugar
  1½ c. flour

1 c. uncooked oatmeal
1 c. melted butter

Combine and cook sugar, clear jell, water and rhubarb. Press half of crumbs in bottom of pan, add rhubarb, then rest of crumbs. Sprinkle with cinnamon.

Apple Goodie

2 qt. peeled and sliced apples
¼ c. sugar
⅛ c. flour

⅛ c. water
½ tsp. cinnamon

Crumbs:
  1 c. oatmeal
  1 c. brown sugar

1 c. flour
⅓ c. soft butter

Mix together apples, sugar, flour, water and cinnamon. Mix crumbs and put on top of apples. Bake at 350° for 45 min. Serve warm with milk or cold with vanilla ice cream. Delicious!

Apple Dumplings

1½ c. sugar
1½ c. water
¼ tsp. cinnamon
¼ tsp. nutmeg
3 Tbsp. butter
½ tsp. red food coloring

2 c. flour
2 tsp. baking powder
1 tsp. salt
⅓ c. shortening
½ c. milk
6 apples, pared and sliced

Cook sugar, water, cinnamon and nutmeg; add butter and food coloring and set aside. Sift flour, baking powder and salt; add shortening. Mix and add milk. Roll into 6 circles. Fill with apples. Sprinkle with cinnamon and sugar, dot with butter and pour cooked mixture over dumplings. Bake in a 9" x 13" x 2" pan at 375° for 15 min. Reduce temperature to 325° and bake 30 min. longer or until apples are done.

Brown Sugar Dumplings

Syrup:
¾ c. brown sugar
1 c. water

2 Tbsp. butter

Batter:
1 c. flour
1 tsp. baking powder
½ tsp. salt
3 Tbsp. sugar

3 Tbsp. butter
½ tsp. vanilla
½ c. milk

Boil syrup ingredients 3 min. Batter: Work butter into the dry ingredients as for pie crumbs. Add vanilla and milk and stir until smooth. Drop batter by spoonfuls into hot syrup and bake 30 - 40 min.

Cinnamon Flop

1 c. white sugar
1 c. milk
2 c. flour

3 Tbsp. soft butter
2 tsp. baking powder

Topping:
1 tsp. cinnamon
1/2 c. melted butter

1/2 c. brown sugar

Cream sugar and butter. Then add milk. Next add baking powder and flour. Mix well. Pour in cake pan and bake at 350° for 20 min. After baking, quickly sprinkle cinnamon and brown sugar on top. Then pour 1/2 c. melted butter over this. Bake at least 10 min. longer. Serve warm with milk.

Pumpkin Roll

Cake:
3 eggs
1 c. sugar
2/3 c. pumpkin
2 tsp. cinnamon

1 tsp. lemon juice
3/4 c. flour
1 tsp. baking powder
1/2 tsp. salt

Filling:
1 c. 10x sugar
4 Tbsp. butter

8 oz. softened cream cheese
1/2 tsp. vanilla

Beat eggs at high speed for 5 min. Mix in the rest of the ingredients. Grease and flour jelly roll pan. Bake at 375° for 15 min. only. Cool 5 min. and turn upside down on towel sprinkled with 10x sugar. Store in refrigerator after putting filling on roll. (Use a linen tea towel so you don't get a lot of fuzz on cakes.)

Happiness is enjoying the little things in life. 🍃

Jelly Roll (Yellow)

¾ c. flour
¾ tsp. baking powder
¼ tsp. salt

4 eggs
¾ c. sugar
1 tsp. vanilla

Sift dry ingredients together. Beat egg whites until stiff. Add egg yolks and mix well. Gradually add sugar and beat until light colored. Add vanilla. Fold in flour. Line a 15" x 10" pan with wax paper. Spread batter evenly. Bake at 400° for 12 min. Turn cake onto a cloth sprinkled with 10x sugar. Remove paper and roll cake and cloth. Unroll again. Add your favorite filling and roll up.

Chocolate Jelly Roll

5 egg yolks, beaten
1 c. 10x sugar
¼ c. fine flour, sifted
5 stiffly beaten egg whites

½ tsp. salt
3 Tbsp. cocoa
1 tsp. vanilla

Add egg whites last and fold lightly to rest of ingredients. Bake at 350° for 10 - 12 min. Dump on lightly (10x) sugared cloth.

Filling:
  1 c. milk
  1 Tbsp. cornstarch
  ½ c. Crisco

¼ c. butter
1 c. 10x sugar

Boil the milk and cornstarch and stir until thickened. Cool. Cream the Crisco, butter and 10x sugar. Add cornstarch mixture to Crisco mixture one teaspoon at a time and beat until fluffy.

Ice Cream Roll

1 angel food cake mix

1 qt. ice cream (any flavor)

Make cake as directed. Line 2 oblong pans with waxed paper. Divide batter into pans. Bake at 350° for 20 min. Let cool 5 min., remove from pans, pull off waxed paper and cool again 5 min. Spoon ice cream on top and roll as a jelly roll. Wrap in aluminum foil and freeze for 6 hrs.

Ice Cream

6 eggs
2 c. sugar
1 tsp. salt
2 cans Carnation milk

5 Tbsp. vanilla
4 Tbsp. Knox gelatin,
    dissolved in $2/3$ c. water

Heat 1 qt. milk and stir gelatin in milk. Add rest of ingredients and beat very well. Add just enough milk until freezer is $3/4$ full. Makes 6 qts.

Banana Split

2 pkgs. graham crackers
2 - 3 bananas
$1/2$ gal. 3-flavored ice-cream
1 c. chopped nuts
1 c. chocolate chips

$1/2$ c. butter
2 c. powdered sugar
$1 1/2$ c. evaporated milk
1 tsp. vanilla
1 pt. whipped cream

Press crumbs in an 11" x 15" pan. Reserve 1 c. for topping. Slice bananas, put over crust. Slice ice cream in $1/2$" thick slices, put over bananas. Sprinkle nuts over ice cream. Freeze till firm. Melt chips and butter. Add sugar and milk. Cook mixture until thick and smooth, stirring constantly. Remove from heat, add vanilla. Cool chocolate mixture, pour over ice cream and sprinkle with remaining graham cracker crumbs. Get out of freezer 10 min. before you eat.

Oreo Cookie Dessert

Oreo cookies, crushed
Cool Whip
1 c. 10x sugar
8 oz. cream cheese

3 c. milk
1 pkg. instant vanilla pudding
1 pkg. instant chocolate pudding

First Layer: Mix well crushed cookies and 6 Tbsp. melted butter. Put in pan.
Second Layer: Mix well 1 c. Cool Whip with sugar and cream cheese.
Third Layer: Mix vanilla and chocolate pudding with milk. Top with Cool Whip and sprinkle with cookie crumbs.

Creamy Pudding

6½ c. milk
¾ c. brown sugar
¾ c. white sugar

3 Tbsp. flour
3 Tbsp. cornstarch
3 eggs

Heat 6 c. milk. Beat eggs. Add sugar, flour and cornstarch. Then add ½ c. milk. Slowly add to heated milk. Stir constantly until thickened. When cool, add a little Cool Whip. Beat often while cooling.

Graham Cracker Pudding

1 lg. pkg. instant vanilla pudding
10 oz. Cool Whip

1 c. graham cracker crumbs

Make pudding according to directions. Allow to set. Stir in graham cracker crumbs and whipped topping. Garnish with more topping and crumbs.

Cherry Pudding

1 qt. fruit
½ c. sugar

2 c. water

Thicken fruit and put in cake pan.

Batter:
1 c. brown sugar
2 eggs
½ c. milk
2 c. flour

1 tsp. baking powder
Vanilla
½ c. shortening

Pour batter on top of fruit. Bake at 350° for 40 min. Serve warm with milk.

Linda's Pudding

3 c. milk
1 c. sugar
3 eggs, separated
2½ Tbsp. cornstarch

¼ tsp. salt
1 Tbsp. butter
1 tsp. vanilla

Mix together and bring to a boil. Stir constantly.

Topping:
3 egg whites
5 Tbsp. sugar

1 oz. melted chocolate

Beat egg whites till stiff. Add sugar and chocolate. Continue beating a few more minutes.

Baked Cup Custard

4 eggs
½ c. sugar
¼ tsp. salt

4 c. milk
½ tsp. vanilla

Beat eggs. Add sugar, salt and vanilla. Scald milk and add to mixture. Stir thoroughly. Pour into custard cups, filling ⅔ full. Sprinkle with nutmeg. Set in hot water to bake. Bake at 400° for 10 min. then at 350° until done. Makes 8 custard cups.

Pumpkin Torte

3 c. crushed graham crackers
⅓ c. sugar
½ c. butter, melted
2 eggs
¾ c. sugar
8 oz. cream cheese
2 c. pumpkin
3 egg yolks

½ c. sugar
½ c. milk
½ tsp. salt
1 Tbsp. cinnamon
1 Tbsp. unflavored gelatin
¼ c. cold water
3 egg whites
¼ c. sugar

Mix grahams, ⅓ c. sugar and butter. Press into a 9" x 13" cake pan. Mix eggs, ¾ c. sugar and cream cheese and pour over crust. Bake 20 min. at 350°. Cook pumpkin, egg yolks, ½ c. sugar, milk, salt and cinnamon until mixture thickens.

Pretzel Treat

1 18-oz. bag broken pretzels
¾ c. oil
1 pkg. Virginal Ranch dressing dry mix

1 tsp. lemon pepper seasoning
1 tsp. garlic powder

Place pretzels in a 9" x 13" pan. Mix ingredients; pour over pretzels. Place in 200° oven for 1 hr. stirring every 15 min.

Eclair Dessert

6 c. milk
6 egg yolks
3 Tbsp. flour (heaping)
3 Tbsp. cornstarch (heaping)

1½ c. sugar
½ c. brown sugar
1 8-oz. container Cool Whip

Heat milk. Beat egg yolks well. Mix together flour and cornstarch then add some milk. Then mix altogether except for Cool Whip. Add Cool Whip when mixture is cooled. Lay grahams in bottom of pan. Put half of pudding on and crackers on top again. Add rest of pudding on top. Add grahams on top and put icing on.

Icing:
3 Tbsp. cocoa
2 Tbsp. oil
2 tsp. cornstarch
2 tsp. vanilla

3 Tbsp. butter or margarine, soft
3 Tbsp. milk
1½ c. 10x sugar

Put on grahams as soon as icing comes to a boil.

Twinkies

1 cake mix
4 eggs
½ c. oil

1 pkg. instant vanilla pudding
1 c. water

Mix all ingredients together. Place in greased 13" x 9" x 2" pan. Bake at 350° for 25 - 30 min. When baked cut apart and put icing in middle. Cut in squares and wrap individually in Saran Wrap.

Strawberry Angel Cake Dessert

½ angel food cake
1 box instant vanilla pudding
1 c. cold milk
1 pt. vanilla ice cream

1 box strawberry jello
1 c. boiling water
10 oz. frozen strawberries

Break cake in small pieces in an 8" x 12" dish. Dissolve pudding in milk. Add ice cream and beat until well mixed. Pour over cake. (Do not stir.) Let set. Dissolve jello in boiling water. Add strawberries. Stir until it begins to thicken. Pour over cake. Do not stir.

Baked Cheesecake

Bottom Part:
  1½ c. graham cracker crumbs
  ⅛ lb. melted butter

1 Tbsp. sugar

Batter:
  4 eggs
  1¼ c. sugar

24 oz. cream cheese
1 tsp. vanilla

Top Part:
  ½ c. sugar
  1 pt. sour cream

1 tsp. vanilla

Put crumbs in pan. Pour batter on top. Bake at 350° for 30 min. Pour top on and bake 10 - 15 min. longer.

Cheese Cake

Crumb Crust:
  2 c. graham cracker crumbs
  1 stick butter, melted
  1 Tbsp. sugar

Batter:
  1 can chilled evaporated milk
  1 pkg. lemon jello
  8 oz. cream cheese
  1 c. sugar

Mix crumbs and press in cake pan. Save some for topping. Beat milk in a large bowl until thick. Mix jello according to directions. Beat in cream cheese while jello is still warm, add sugar and beat everything together. Pour in pan and sprinkle with remaining crumbs. Refrigerate at least 2 hrs. before serving.

Cherry Cheese Cupcakes

Kasche

3 pkg. cream cheese
²/₃ c. sugar
3 eggs

1 Tbsp. vanilla
Vanilla wafers
1 can pie filling

Mix all ingredients except wafers and pie filling. Place a wafer in the bottom of each cupcake paper. Fill ³/₄ full with cheese mixture. Bake at 350° for 15 min. Cool and top with pie filling.

Cream Filled Cupcakes

4 c. flour
1 c. cocoa
2 tsp. soda
2 tsp. baking powder
2 tsp. vanilla
1 c. Wesson oil

2¹/₂ c. sugar
1 tsp. salt
2¹/₄ c. coffee (ready to drink)
4 egg yolks
4 egg whites, beat and add last

Filling:
   1 c. milk
   1 Tbsp. cornstarch
   ¹/₂ c. Crisco

¹/₄ c. butter
1 c. sugar

Boil milk and cornstarch. Cool, then add rest of ingredients and beat until fluffy.

Short Cake

1 c. white sugar
¹/₂ c. shortening
1 egg, separated

¹/₂ c. sweet milk
1³/₄ c. flour
1 tsp. baking powder

Cream sugar and shortening until smooth. Beat egg yolk with 1 Tbsp. of the milk, add and stir until well blended. Sift flour and baking powder and add alternately with milk. Add well beaten egg white last. Bake in moderate oven. Serve hot with cold milk or other fruit.

Jimmy Carter Dessert

1 c. flour
1 stick oleo
2/3 c. chopped nuts
1/3 c. peanut butter
8 oz. cream cheese

1 c. confectioners sugar
9 oz. Cool Whip
1 pkg. instant vanilla pudding
1 pkg. instant chocolate pudding
2 3/4 c. milk

Mix together oleo, nuts and flour. (Save some nuts for the top.) Press into a 13" x 9" pan. Bake at 350° for 20 min. Let cool. Cream together peanut butter, cream cheese, sugar and 1 c. Cool Whip. Mix puddings and milk. Spread peanut butter layer on crust, then put pudding mixture on. Spread remaining Cool Whip on top, then sprinkle chopped nuts on top. Refrigerate.

Hawaiian Dessert

1 yellow cake mix
3 (3.4 oz.) pkgs. instant vanilla pudding
4 c. cold milk
1 1/2 tsp. coconut extract

8 oz. cream cheese
20 oz. crushed pineapple, drained
2 c. heavy cream
2 c. flaked coconut, toasted

Mix cake mix according to directions. Pour into 2 13" x 9" x 2" pans. Bake at 350° till done. Cool completely. Mix puddings and milk and extract. Beat 2 min., add cream cheese and beat well. Stir in pineapple. Spread over the cooled cakes. Whip and sweeten cream to put on top and sprinkle with coconut. Chill at least 2 hrs. Prepared dessert can be covered and frozen for up to 1 month. Very simple and delicious.

Lemon Supreme

1 c. walnuts
1/4 lb. butter
8 oz. cream cheese
2 pkgs. pudding mix (any flavor)

1 c. flour
1 c. Cool Whip
1/2 c. powdered sugar

Mix the walnuts, flour and butter. Then press into a 13" x 9" cake pan and bake 15 min. at 350°. Combine the Cool Whip, cream cheese and sugar. Spread on crust. Mix the pudding for the top. Chill and garnish with Cool Whip and walnuts.

Lemon Fruit Freeze

²/₃ c. butter
¹/₃ c. sugar
7 c. Rice Krispies
14 oz. condensed milk

¹/₂ c. Real lemon juice
21 oz. lemon pie filling
2 c. whipped cream

Mix butter, sugar and Rice Krispies. Press into a 9" x 13" cake pan. Bake 12 min. at 300°. Mix milk, juice, pie filling and whipped cream. Put on crust. Freeze. Take out of freezer 30 min. before serving.

Pink Stuff

20 lg. marshmallows
2 c. miniature marshmallows
1 c. boiling water
1 lg. box jello, strawberry or raspberry

1 can crushed pineapple
8 oz. cream cheese
1 pkg. Dream Whip
1 tray ice cubes

Dissolve jello in boiling water. Add marshmallows and cream cheese. Place this over low heat on stove, stirring until dissolved. Remove from burner, add crushed pineapples, including juice. Add tray of ice cubes, cool until well set, but not firm. Prepare Dream Whip and fold into jello. Place in refrigerator until chilled and firm.

Jello Tapioca

1 qt. warm water
1 c. sugar
¹/₂ c. minute tapioca

¹/₂ c. jello (any flavor)
Cool Whip and fruit

Bring to a boil the warm water, sugar and tapioca. Add the jello. Cool, then add Cool Whip and fruit.

Finger Jello

3 boxes (pt. size) jello
4 Tbsp. Knox gelatin

4 c. boiling water

Let set till firm, cut in pieces and eat with fingers.

Rainbow Finger Jello

1½ c. jello (any flavor)
4 Tbsp. plain gelatin

4 c. boiling water

Combine jello, gelatin and water. Stir until dissolved then add 2 c. cold water. Pour into 2 13" x 9" cake pans. Refrigerate until firm. Then mix:

1 c. boiling water

2 Tbsp. plain gelatin

Dissolve, then add:

1 c. evaporated milk

3 Tbsp. sugar

Pour on top of first mixture. When firm make another mixture of the above jello recipe, but a different color.

Orange Dessert

1 qt. water
1 pkg. orange Kool-Aid

½ c. clear jell
1¼ c. sugar

Bring these to boil. Cool. Add mandarin oranges.

Fruit Pizza

2 c. flour
2 sticks butter
2 Tbsp. sugar

Press on pizza pan and prick with fork. Bake at 350° for 15 min. or until brown.

Filling:
1 lg. Cool Whip container
16 oz. cream cheese
3/4 c. 10x sugar
2 Tbsp. milk

Spread on cooled crust and top with fresh or canned fruit.

Fruit Dip

8 oz. cream cheese
1 c. marshmallow creme
8 oz. whipped topping
1/4 c. dry jello (any flavor)

Mix well and dip any kind of fruit.

Lemon Squares

Crust:
1 c. butter
2 c. flour
1/2 c. 10x sugar
Dash of salt

Filling:
4 eggs
2 c. sugar
1/4 c. flour
6 Tbsp. lemon juice
1 tsp. baking powder

Crust: Combine all ingredients and press into a greased 9" x 13" pan. Bake at 350° for 15 min. and set aside.

Filling: Combine eggs and sugar; beat well. Add flour, lemon juice, and baking powder. Pour over crust and bake at 350° for 20 min. When cool, sprinkle with 10x sugar and serve.

Pecan Pick-Ups

3 oz. cream cheese   1 stick oleo
1 c. flour

Mix till smooth, form into 24 small balls and chill. Press into muffin pans to form pastry-like shell.

Filling:
 3/4 c. brown sugar   1 Tbsp. butter
 1 egg   1 tsp. vanilla
 1/2 c. pecans

Mix well and put 1 tsp. filling in each shell and bake at 350° for 25-30 min.

Raisin Mumbles

Crumbs:
 3/4 c. margarine   1 c. brown sugar
 1 1/2 c. oatmeal   1/2 tsp. salt
 1/2 tsp. soda   1 3/4 c. flour

Filling:
 2 1/2 c. raisins   1/2 c. sugar
 2 Tbsp. cornstarch   3 Tbsp. lemon juice
 3/4 c. water

Cook filling ingredients together. Press half of crumbs in cake pan. Put filling on and sprinkle rest of crumbs on top. Bake at 350° for 30 - 35 min.

Mother's Chocolate Chip Bars

1/2 c. soft margarine   1 3/4 c. flour
1 1/2 c. brown sugar   1 1/2 tsp. baking powder
2 lg. eggs   1 c. chocolate chips
1 tsp. vanilla

Put in buttered 9" x 13" cake pan. Bake at 350° for 30 min.

Caramel Pop Corn

2 c. brown sugar
2 sticks margarine
1/2 c. corn syrup

1 tsp. salt
1 tsp. soda
1 tsp. vanilla

Boil ingredients 5 min. Pour over 6 qt. unsalted popped corn. Bake 1 hr. at 200°. Stir every 15 min.

Puffed Wheat Squares

1/2 c. butter
1/2 c. corn syrup
1/2 c. brown sugar

4 tsp. cocoa, optional
7 c. puffed wheat

Melt first 3 ingredients together. Then add puffed wheat. Press into buttered pans.

Rice Crispy Treats

1/4 c. butter
5 c. Rice Crispies cereal

1/2 lb. marshmallows

Melt butter and marshmallows in double boiler over hot water. Then pour mixture over rice crispies and press in a buttered pan. Let cool, then cut in blocks.

Cream Taffy

1 pt. white corn syrup
1 Tbsp. gelatin
Paraffin (size of walnut)

2 lb. white sugar
1 pt. cream
1 Tbsp. vanilla

Combine all ingredients except gelatin. Boil till a hard ball forms. Soak gelatin in 1/2 c. cold water and add just before removing from heat. Cool, then it's ready to pull.

Creamy Fudge

3 c. granulated sugar
3 Tbsp. margarine
3 Tbsp. light corn syrup
1/8 tsp. salt

1 c. cream
1 sq. semi-sweet chocolate, cut up
1 tsp. vanilla
1/2 c. chopped nuts, optional

Peanut Butter Cups

1/2 c. margarine
1 Tbsp. hot milk
2 c. marshmallow creme
2 Tbsp. Crisco

2 Tbsp. flour
1 Tbsp. vanilla
1 lb. 10x sugar
12 oz. peanut butter

Shape into balls and dip in chocolate.

Peanut Butter Eggs

1/2 lb. margarine
2 c. peanut butter
1 1/2 lb. confectioners sugar

1 1/2 tsp. vanilla
6 oz. semi-sweet chocolate
1 oz. paraffin (if desired)

Cream together margarine, 1 c. peanut butter and vanilla. Add sugar, mix thoroughly. Carefully blend in remaining cup of peanut butter. Form into balls. Melt chocolate and paraffin in double boiler. Dip balls in chocolate using a toothpick or fork. Place on waxed paper.

Crunch Bars

1/2 c. butter
3/4 c. granulated sugar
2 eggs
1 tsp. vanilla

3/4 c. flour
1/4 tsp. baking powder
1/4 tsp. salt

Mix all ingredients well and put into a 9" x 13" pan. It will be a small amount of batter. Bake at 350° approx. 15 min. Do not overbake. As soon as you take it out of oven cover bottom part with miniature marshmallows. Let melt and partially cool. Next melt 1 c. peanut butter and 6 oz. chocolate chips. Mix well. Add 1 1/2 c. rice crispies. Spread on top of marshmallows. Cool and cut in squares.

Breakfast and Jellies

❧

Come In

Come in! But don't expect to find
All dishes done, all floors ashine;
See crumpled rugs, the toys galore
The smudged, fingerprinted door.
The little ones we shelter here
Don't thrive in spotless atmosphere;
They're most inclined to disarray
And carefree, even messy play.

Their needs are great, patience small;
All days I'm at their beck and call.
It's "Mommie, come!," "Mommie, see!"
Wiggly worms and red scraped knee,
Painted pictures, blocks piled high
My floors unshined, the days go by.
Some future day they'll flee this nest
And I at last will have a rest.
And which really matters more—
A happy child, or a polished floor?

**Breakfast
and Jellies**

❧

Dirty Dishes

Thank God for dirty dishes,
They have a tale to tell;
While other folks go hungry,
We are eating very well.
With home and health and happiness
We shouldn't want to fuss
For by the stack of evidence
God's very good to us.

Breakfast Varieties

Ham and eggs served with stewed crackers.

Scrambled eggs and toast served with bacon.

Eggs over light served on buttered toast with sausage.

Poached eggs served on stewed crackers with toast and jelly.

Pancakes and scrambled eggs with bacon.

Cooked oatmeal.

Country Brunch

16 pieces firm white bread
1 lb. sliced ham
16 oz. mozzarella and cheddar cheese
6 eggs

3 c. milk
$\frac{1}{2}$ tsp. mustard
$\frac{1}{8}$ tsp. onion powder

Topping:
   $\frac{1}{2}$ c. melted butter
   3 c. corn flakes or bread crumbs

Grease 13" x 9" x 2" baking pan and layer as follows: Cover bottom of pan with half of bread, half of ham, and half of cheese. Repeat layers. Combine eggs, milk and seasoning. Pour over bread. Refrigerate 30 min. before baking. Combine topping. Sprinkle over top. Bake at 350° for 45 min. Cover with foil, let stand 15 min.

Breakfast Strata

12 eggs
1/4 tsp. pepper

1/2 tsp. salt
1/2 c. milk

White Sauce:
  2 Tbsp. butter
  1 1/2 c. milk

1 Tbsp. flour
Cheese

Mix eggs, seasonings and milk well. Then scramble. Pour in casserole dish. Cook white sauce then add cheese, stir until melted. Add to eggs. Bake at 350° for 30 min. Serve with toast and bacon.

Home Style Mush

2 3/4 c. water
1 c. cornmeal

3/4 tsp. salt

Cook this mixture together over low heat for 30 min. Pour in flat pan 2" deep. Cool and refrigerate. Slice in 1/2" pieces and fry on both sides in lard or Crisco. This can be served with honey or syrup.

Cheese Biscuits

1 1/2 c. all-purpose flour
1/2 tsp. soda
3/4 c. sour milk or buttermilk

1/2 tsp. salt
4 Tbsp. shortening
1 c. grated cheese

Sift, then measure flour. Sift again with soda and salt. Rub in shortening. Add cheese to this mixture. Add sour milk, stirring quickly to form a soft dough. Drop by teaspoons onto a baking sheet. Bake in at 475° for 12 min. Serve with eggs.

Cheese Omelet

2 level Tbsp. melted butter
3 level Tbsp. flour
1/2 tsp. soda

1/4 c. cheese, cut fine
3 eggs, beaten
1/2 c. scalded milk

Mix the above ingredients and bake at 350° for 50 - 55 min.

Delicious Pancakes

5 egg yolks
1 c. milk
1 c. flour
Pinch of salt
5 egg whites, beaten stiff

1 Tbsp. sugar
2 tsp. baking powder (heaping)
2 Tbsp. butter, melted over hot
    water

Beat egg yolks and milk together, add dry ingredients which have been sifted together, then melted butter. Fold in egg whites just before baking. Have griddle hot.

Whole Wheat Pancakes

3/4 c. whole wheat flour
1 Tbsp. sugar
1 tsp. baking powder
1/2 tsp. soda

1 c. milk
1/2 tsp. salt
1 egg
2 Tbsp. oil

Pancake Syrup

4 c. white sugar
1/2 c. brown sugar
1 c. water

1 tsp. vanilla
1 tsp. maple flavoring

Boil 10 min. Then add vanilla and flavoring.

Granola Cereal

2 sticks butter or margarine
2 c. brown sugar
1/2 c. honey or molasses

2 Tbsp. vanilla
12 c. oatmeal
2 c. raisins

Melt the butter or margarine. Add the remaining ingredients. Put in cake pans and bake at 250° for 1 hr., stirring occasionally. Store in an airtight container.

Breakfast Granola

10 c. oatmeal
2 c. wheat germ
2 c. brown sugar
1 c. coconut
2 c. crushed cashews
2 c. powdered milk

3/4 c. butter
1 c. honey
1 tsp. salt
1 tsp. cinnamon
1 tsp. vanilla
Chopped dates or raisins, optional

Combine oatmeal, wheat germ, brown sugar and powdered milk. Mix well. Melt butter. Add honey, salt, vanilla and cinnamon. Pour over oatmeal mixture and mix very well. Spread on cookie sheets and roast at 275° for 30 min. Stir a couple of times while roasting. Remove from oven and add coconut, raisins and cashews. Cool and store in tight container.

Grape Nuts

1 pt. molasses
2 pts. buttermilk
6 c. graham flour

2 tsp. soda
Salt

Put a 1" thick layer into 9" x 13" cake pans. Bake as you would a cake. 375° approx. 45 - 60 min. Let dry out overnight then put through a grinder. Toast in a slow oven until done.

French Toast

Beat 2 eggs, add ¾ c. milk. Dip pieces of bread in the mixture. Melt and lightly brown butter in a pan. Put in the bread pieces and sprinkle with salt. Fry until brown on both sides.

White American Cheese Spread
(For our church dinner)

2 ⅔ c. milk
1 stick butter
½ tsp. salt

40 slices white American cheese
½ tsp. soda

Heat milk until almost boiling. Add butter and soda and salt; remove from heat. Add cheese. Stir until dissolved. Put plastic wrap on top against cheese until it's cooled, so it doesn't form a skin on top.

Apple Butter

1 gal. applesauce
6 c. sugar
2 c. cider

8 tsp. cinnamon
1 tsp. cloves

Simmer for 3 hrs.

Apple Butter
(Oven method)

7 lb. apples (16 c.)
3 lb. brown sugar

1 c. vinegar or cider
2 Tbsp. cinnamon

Cook apples until soft and put through sieve. Add remaining ingredients and put into a pan with lid in oven. Bake 3 hrs. at 350°. Stir occasionally. Pour into jars and seal. Makes 5 qt.

Black Raspberry Jam

3 qt. raspberries
4 c. juice

1 pkg. Jel-ease fruit pectin
5½ c. sugar

Wash, crush and simmer about 5 min., covered. Squeeze out juice through cloth or bag. Put juice into 6 - 8 qt. saucepan. Stir Jel-ease (or sure jell) into juice. Place on heat and stir continuously while bringing to a full boil. Gradually add the sugar, stirring well to dissolve it.

Rhubarb Jam

5 c. rhubarb (cut very fine)
1 sm. pkg. strawberry jello

4 c. sugar

Let the rhubarb and sugar stand overnight. In the morning, boil 5 min., then add the jello. Boil 3 min. after dry jello is added. Do not can for winter use, just enjoy it fresh.

Pineapple Jelly

1½ lb. sugar
1 qt. crushed pineapple

5 lb. white Karo syrup

Cook 30 min. only or it will get too stiff.

Apricot Jelly

2 c. apricots
1 c. apples
1 c. water

3½ c. sugar
¼ tsp. alum

Bring to a boil water, apples and apricots. Add sugar and alum and boil 20 min.

Old Fashioned Jelly

5 lb. sugar
1 gal. light Karo

2 qt. strawberries, or other fruit

Cook 20 min. and jar. Gives a good sticky jelly.

Red Beet Jelly

6 c. beet juice
1/2 c. lemon juice
2 boxes sure jell

8 c. sugar
6 oz. pkg. jello, raspberry or
   strawberry

Combine first 3 ingredients and bring to a hard boil. Add sugar and jello and boil 6 - 8 min. longer.

Cooked Peanut Butter Spread

5 c. brown sugar
4 c. granulated sugar
1¹/₃ c. molasses

4 c. water
5 lb. peanut butter
1 qt. marshmallow creme

Boil sugars, molasses and water a few min., then cool. Add peanut butter and marshmallow creme. Mix very well.

Thankful for What?

"Why are you so thankful, Hubby?"
My "better half" asked me last night.
Then she laughed because I told her—
Thankful for my appetite."

Preserving Foods

≈

Mother

True and noble, sweet and loving
　Dearest friend on earth I know;
Ever patient and forgiving,
　Loving me where'er I go.

Never idle, never shirking,
　Blessed be her toil worn hands;
Carefree never, always working,
　Giving more than right demands.

Never doubting, always trusting,
　Hoping for a better day;
Always cheerful and consoling,
　Wiping tears and cares away.

Oh, how sweet the name of mother,
　Yet how oft she's made to grieve
When a wayward son or daughter
　Her wise counsel won't receive.

Why not do our best for mother
　While she's with us here below?
E'en our best can ne'er repay her
　All the debt of love we owe.

Sacrifice so great and noble
　For our being she has made;
Friend in joy and friend in sorrow,
　Never will her friendship fade.

In making pickles, use white vinegar to make clear pickles and coarse salt which comes in 5 lb. bags. This is not rock salt.

Avoid using iodized salt for pickle making.

Most pickles are better if allowed to stand six weeks before using.

Seven Day Sweet Pickles

30 cucumbers (4" long and fairly thin)
1 qt. vinegar
1 qt. water

16 c. sugar
$1/4$ c. mixed spices
$1/4$ c. salt

Place washed cucumbers in a crock or stainless pail or dish. Cover with freshly boiling water. Let stand 24 hrs. Drain and again cover with boiling water. Continue until they have 4 hot water baths.

The fifth day, drain, rinse and slice cucumbers into $1/4$" slices. Combine vinegar, sugar, salt and spices tied in a bag and bring to a boil. Pour over slices. Let stand 24 hrs. Pour off syrup. Reheat to boiling and pour over agin. Repeat 2 more days.

The ninth day, drain and reheat syrup. Pack slices in jars and cover with hot syrup. Seal at once. Makes approximately 8 pts.

Fourteen Day Sweet Pickles

First day: Wash 2 gal. cucumbers; cut to size or use whole. Cover with salt water that is strong enough to float an egg, that it, 2 c. to the gallon of cold water. Stir every day for seven days.

Eighth day: Drain pickles. Cover with fresh boiling water.

Ninth day: Same as above, adding 3 Tbsp. alum to the water.

Tenth day: Drain. Add boiling water. Cool and drain again. Cover with a hot vinegar syrup made thus: Tie in a muslin spice bag 2 Tbsp. whole mixed pickling spice, 1 Tbsp. whole allspice, 1 Tbsp. celery seed and 1/2 oz. cinnamon sticks. Combine 2 qt. vinegar, 1 qt. water and 2 c. sugar. Bring to a boil the syrup with the spice bag.

Eleventh day: Drain off vinegar. Boil with spice bag and 2 c. sugar and return to pickles.

Twelfth day: Same as previous day, adding 2 more c. of sugar.

Thirteenth day: Same as twelfth day.

Fourteenth day: Pack pickles into cans and cover with boiling syrup. Seal.

If you are looking for crisp pickle, this is it. The processing is really more fun than bother.

Sweet Dill Pickles

2 c. water
2 c. vinegar
3 c. sugar
2 Tbsp. salt

Dill
Sliced onions
Sliced garlic bulb

Pack jars with pickles. Heat first 4 ingredients and pour over pickles. Put 1 head dill, 1 slice onion and 1 slice garlic on top of jar. Cold pack 5 min.

Kosher Dill Pickles

1/2 tsp. alum
1/4 tsp. salt

1 Tbsp. Kosher dill pickle mix

Put on top of each quart with pickles.

8 c. water
4 c. vinegar

2 c. sugar

Cook syrup and pour over pickles. To cold pack bring only to boiling point then remove from heat.

Mustard Pickles

1 qt. vinegar to 3 qt. water
1/2 c. ground mustard
1 Tbsp. saccharin

1/2 c. whole allspice
1 tsp. alum
1/2 c. salt

Bring liquid to boiling, then add small whole cucumbers. Let them change color. Then jar and add boiling liquid. Seal.

Banana Pickles

2 c. vinegar
1 c. water
3 c. sugar
1 tsp. salt

1 tsp. celery seed
1 tsp. mustard seed
1 tsp. tumeric (if desired; gives
　　more color)

Bring to a boil, then pour over long thinly sliced cucumbers. Cold pack 15 min. in jar.

Bread and Butter Pickles

1 gal. thin sliced pickles
2 c. sliced onions
1/4 c. salt
4 1/2 c. sugar

1 tsp. tumeric
2 Tbsp. mustard seed
2 c. vinegar
A little water

Slice cucumbers. Add onions and salt. Mix well and let stand 3 hrs. Drain dry. Make juice and bring to a boil. Add pickles and bring to a good boil. Put in jars and seal.

Saccharin Pickles

2 c. water
2 c. vinegar

2 Tbsp. salt
2 Tbsp. sugar

Bring to a boil. Add 1/4 tsp. saccharin. Pack in jars and boil for 3 - 5 min. Makes 2 qts.

Sweets and Sours

You cannot separate the Dutchman from his sweets and sours. There are a few who even want them on the breakfast table. Somewhere through the years, some hausfra may have served precisely seven sweets and seven sours on her table but most scholars today accept this as a myth. However, we do crave our pickled fruits and vegetables to spice our hearty fare.

Pickle Relish

4 qt. pickles
1 qt. onions
½ qt. peppers
3 tsp. salt
2 tsp. mustard seed

1 tsp. tumeric
2 tsp. celery seed
2 lb. sugar
2 c. vinegar

Grind pickles, onions and peppers. Add salt and let stand 3 hrs., then drain. Cook everything and simmer 3 min. Put in jars and seal. Makes 9 pts. (Zucchini can be used instead of pickles.)

Pickled Cauliflower and Carrots

Cook desired amount of vegetables and mix after being cooled. Pack into jars and add syrup.

4 c. sugar
1 Tbsp. salt

2½ c. water
2 c. vinegar

Cook until sugar is dissolved. Cold pack 10 min. A slice of hot pepper can be added to each jar to give them a "hot" flavor.

Sweet Peppers

3 c. sugar
1 c. vinegar

2 c. water
Pinch of salt

Just heat until it's syrup or boils. Cold pack 10 - 15 min. I use sweet banana peppers and slice them like an onion ring. They look like the boughten sweet peppers you sometimes get with subs. Makes a good sandwich!

Pepper and Cabbage Slaw

1 c. sugar
1 c. water

3 Tbsp. vinegar

Grind cabbage through a food chopper. Dice peppers real fine. Mix and put in jars. Cook water mixture to dissolve sugar. This is enough for 1 qt. Cold pack 20 min. This recipe is good for small stuffing peppers, too.

Pickled Onion Rings

8 c. sliced onions (about 3 lbs.)
Boiling water
1 c. white vinegar

1 c. sugar
2 tsp. canning salt
$1/2$ tsp. mustard seed

Blanch onions in boiling water for 4 min. Drain. In a large saucepan, combine vinegar, sugar, salt and mustard seed. Bring to a boil. Add onions and simmer for 4 min. Pack into sterilized standard canning jars. Fill to $1/2$" of top, making sure vinegar covers onions. Adjust lids. Process in a boiling water bath for 5 min. Makes 2 - 3 pts. Serve in sandwiches, on relish trays or with roast meat or game.

Very Good Chow Chow

2 c. vinegar
6 c. sugar
2 tsp. mustard, dried

4 c. water
4 tsp. salt
$1/4$ tsp. tumeric

Mix all kinds of vegetables you like. Pour juice over and can. Cold pack for 15 min.

Pickled Red Beets

4 c. beet juice (use water to make 4 c.   4 c. sugar
   if juice is scant)   1 Tbsp. salt
2 c. vinegar

Bring this mixture to a boil. Add cooked, peeled and sliced red beets to the hot juice and bring to a boil again. Jar and seal. (Cylinda beet is a good variety to use for pickling.)

To Cold Pack Cantaloupes

2 c. granulated sugar   1 1/2 tsp. salt
1 qt. water   1 tsp. alum
2/3 c. vinegar

Mix syrup until all sugar is dissolved. Fill jars with cantaloupe balls or square pieces – whichever you prefer. Fill with juice and cold pack for 40 min.

Ketchup

4 qt. tomato juice   2 tsp. celery salt
3 red peppers   2 tsp. mustard
4 onions   1/2 tsp. allspice
2 Tbsp. salt   1/2 tsp. cloves
3 c. sugar   1 tsp. cinnamon
1/2 c. vinegar   1 tsp. paprika

Combine tomato juice, peppers, onions, sugar and spices. Cook 1 hr. Put through sieve. Add vinegar and cook until thick. Then it's ready to jar.

Pizza Sauce

4 qt. tomato juice
1 onion, cut up fine
1 tsp. garlic salt
1 tsp. oregano

1 tsp. black pepper
1/2 tsp. Tabasco sauce
2 Tbsp. salt
2 Tbsp. sugar (heaping)

Cook 1/2 hr., then cold pack 20 min. Thicken with clear jell if needed.

Spaghetti Sauce

6 onions, chopped
2 peppers, chopped
6 qt. tomato juice
6 c. catsup
6 tsp. oregano

2 tsp. garlic powder
6 tsp. salt
3 tsp. pepper
Sugar to taste

Brown onions and peppers in 1/4 c. vegetable oil. Combine all ingredients and simmer to desired thickness. This can be frozen or canned.

Sandwich Spread

6 red peppers
6 green peppers
6 green tomatoes
6 pickles, unpared (green)
6 onions (medium size)

2 c. vinegar
4 c. sugar
1 c. flour
1/2 pt. mustard

Cut vegetables in pieces or strips. Put salt on these and let stand 2 hrs. Drain, then grind in food grinder. Add the vinegar, flour and sugar. Cook 15 min. Add the mustard and cook 5 min. more, stirring constantly, as it scorches easily. Put in jars and cold pack 5 - 10 min. Use on bologna sandwiches.

Time Table for Canning with the Pressure Cooker
(10 lbs. pressure)

Vegetables (Cooking Time)	Min.	Vegetables (Cooking Time)	Min.
Asparagus	40	Peas	40
Beans, String	40	Pumpkin	60
Beans, Shell or Lima	50	Sauerkraut	40
Beets	40	Spinach and other greens	40
Carrots	40	Squash	40
Cauliflower	40	Succotash	50
Corn, whole grain	50	Tomatoes and Corn, equal parts	50
Corn, cream style	60	Meat	105
Parsnips	40	Fish	90

Time Table for Vegetables and Meats in the Hot Water Bath

Vegetables	Min.	Vegetables	Min.
Asparagus	180	Parsnips	40
Beans, String	180	Greens, spinach, etc.	180
Beans, Lima	180	Okra	120
Beets	120	Peas	180
Carrots	120	Pumpkin	240
Cauliflower	120	Squash	180
Corn	180	Vegetable Combinations	180
Corn, cream style	60	Meat	180

Time Table for Canning in the Hot Water Bath
The following foods are most suitable for canning by this process:

	Min.		Min.
Apples	20-30	Peppers	30
Apricots	16	Pineapple	120
Blackberries, dewberries	16	Plums	16
Cherries	16	Quinces	60
Elderberries	16	Raspberries	16
Fruit Juices	20	Rhubarb	16
Grapes	16	Sauerkraut	60
Huckleberries	16	Tomatoes	30
Peaches	20	Tomato Juice	20
Pears	20-30		

Thermometer Readings for Candy

	Degrees
Thread	230-234
Soft ball	234-240
Firm ball	244-248
Hard ball	250-266
Soft crack	270-290
Hard crack	300-310

Syrup for Canning Fruit

Thin	1 part sugar to 3 parts water
Medium	1 part sugar to 2 parts water
Thick	1 part sugar to 1 part water

ε∂

A Recipe for Husbands

Select the best woman you can and brush her carefully to rid her of any indifference. Be careful not to beat her as you would a spoiled child, for beating will make her tough and apt to froth at the mouth.

Lift her gently into the home preserving kettle and tie her with strong cords of affection which are not easily broken. Do not sear her with sarcasm, for that causes spitting and sputtering which may ultimately result in spontaneous combustion. Scramble when difficulties arise.

Do not soak her in liquor either, for excessive draughts will make her mushy and spongy with your friends, and in the United States stewed wives have never been popular.

It is best to let her simmer tenderly at will, to blend tactfully with dressing and seasoning. Humor her before asking a great favor. A little caress or even a glass of cool water will often add to her tenderness.

Flavor her with the oil of happiness, an ounce of understanding and a bushel of laughter and fun.

Should she seem weak or troubled with masculine flirtations, smother her in garlic and onions, and treble your charms.

Need her; and let her knead her dough, and be sure to have some of the dough for the little dumplings.

Do not spoil her disposition by unpleasantness, but serve her daily on a platter of strength and courage, praise her and garnish her with occasional flowers and candy.

Miscellaneous

Recipe for a Boiling Wife

Take: 1 cool, fresh, good natured wife
Add:
4 small children
1 yelping dog
1 cranky neighbor

Stir well, blend in equal parts of heat, humidity, dust and stale air. Baste with annoying interruptions, spilled milk, skinned knees, washing that won't wait, a pile of ironing to do, and jelly smeared on the floor. Top with a splitting headache. Let simmer in a 98° house for 10 hours or until boiling point is reached.

What Is a Mother Made Of?

A little wisdom to help her guide
Her children's steps while they're by her side.
A little patience when they forget
Or haven't learned by experience yet . . .
    That's what a mother is made of.

A little praise for a job well done
A little nonsense, a little fun
A little tenderness from the heart
When a special dream has fallen apart . . .
    That's what a mother is made of.

A little trust from day to day
As her children seek to find their way.
A little faith in the lives they lead
And all the love her children need . . .
    That's what a mother is made of.

Play Dough

1 c. flour
½ c. salt
1 - 2 Tbsp. vegetable oil

2 tsp. cream of tartar
Several drops of food coloring
1 c. water

Combine all in pan and cook over medium heat, 4 - 5 min. or until it forms a ball and does not stick to the pan; cool. Knead well. Put in plastic bag or plastic container with tight lid.

Paste for Children's Scrap Book

1 c. flour
1 c. sugar
1 Tbsp. alum

1 qt. water
3 drops oil of clove

Boil until thick. Keep in refrigerator.

Soap
(For washing clothes)

4 cans Banner lye
1 lb. borax
16 lb. lard

½ lb. rosin
34 qt. water

Cook lye, borax and rosin till dissolved, then add water gradually.

Homemade Bubble Bath

1 c. dish washing detergent
2 c. Epsom salts
Few drops perfume

4 drops glycerine
4 drops food coloring

Mix salts and detergent together in large bowl. Combine the glycerine, coloring, and perfume in a tablespoon before adding to the salt mixture. Mix well and package in bottles.

Spring Tonic for Grapes
(For 1 stalk)

1 gal. water   1 handful salt
1 handful sulfur   1 handful lime

Make a small cavity around the grapevine and pour this over stalk and into the hole.

Plant Food

1 tsp. baking powder   ½ tsp. ammonia
1 tsp. Epsom salt   1 gal. warm water

Bird Feed

1 c. peanut butter   1 c. shortening
4 c. cornmeal   1 c. white flour

Bird Balls

3½ c. oatmeal   3½ c. cornmeal
1 qt. water   3½ c. Cream of Wheat
12 oz. peanut butter

Cook oatmeal in water 2 min. Remove from heat. Stir in lard. Add cornmeal and Cream of Wheat. Cool then form balls.

Attract Chickadees

Roll pinecones in peanut butter and add raisins, nuts, or sunflowers. Hang from trees with a string.

COUNTRY SALE

When it gives a real good sale
    You ought to see the crowd,
There's such a commotion in the field,
    And everything so loud.

The auctioneer he stands right up
    And shows off all the stuff,
And you can bet he don't sell none
    Unless he gets enough.

There's everything was hid away:
    Old guns, and books and shoes,
The attic and cellar is redd out
    For quilts and picture-views.

The people come from far away
    In big machines and small,
Some dressed so awful fancy like
    It wonders me they call.

I seen them buy a butter-mold
    For fifty cents or more
That we could get for twenty cents
    Down at Chon Grumber's store.

They take old dishes all with dust,
    And buy old rusty pans,
And one she glutzed so up and down,
    To get some painted fans.

Yes well, the country sale makes good
    For auctioneer and all,
Enough old stuff gets redd away
    To fill the fire hall.

Some Good Points

Helpful Hints

Cooking Tips

To prevent lumpy gravy add a little salt to the flour before adding the water.

To cool a dish of hot food quickly, set it in a pan of cold water which has been well salted.

When using butter, remember that one stick (a quarter of a pound) is equal to $1/2$ c. when measured.

To prevent hot fat from splattering, sprinkle a little salt, or flour, in it before frying.

Baked beets are more delicious when prepared the same as baked potatoes. They have a sweeter and better taste than when they are boiled.

Instead of greasing a pancake griddle, rub it with a cut raw potato when hot and it will not stick or have an unpleasant odor.

To avoid shelling fresh peas, wash them carefully and cook them as they are. When done the pods will rise to the surface and can easily be skimmed off, which adds to the flavor.

To remove pin feathers easily, take turkey out of oven at the end of the first thirty minutes of roasting and remove with tweezers.

Put lemons in hot water for several minutes before squeezing and they will yield more juice.

To prevent the juices from a berry pie running over in the oven, stick a few short pieces of large macaroni through the center of the top crust.

To remove odor from the pan after frying fish fill pan with vinegar and let come to a boil.

Chop onions without tears by freezing or refrigerating first.

Ripen tomatoes out of direct sunlight, which softens rather than ripens them.

To keep brown sugar soft, store in refrigerator in a plastic bag.

To keep potato slices from discoloring, soak in water to which lemon juice has been added.

Butter around the outside of kettle in which you are cooking jelly to prevent it from running over.

Measure shortening before molasses in baking and it will not stick to the cup.

To measure shortening accurately, fill cup half full of cold water. Put the shortening into the cup until the water comes to the top.

Marshmallows can be cut with ease by using a scissors dipped in hot water.

To brown pies use a small pastry brush and brush with milk before putting in the oven.

A few cloves in the kettle of fat, gives the doughnuts a nice flavor.

For extra juicy, extra nutritious hamburgers, add 1/4 c. evaporated milk per pound of meat before shaping.

Grate 4 tsp. lemon peel. Add to 1/2 c. sugar. You've got lemon sugar to sprinkle into tea, over oatmeal, on french toast, cereal, etc.

Try adding 1 tsp. baking powder to 1 qt. potatoes while mashing them. They will be fluffier.

Would you like to give your children a different dish than just fixing your regular oatmeal? After it is cooked, stir in a few tablespoons of instant chocolate or Nestles Quik. Add just the amount of chocolate to suit your taste. We use it only for special treats now and then.

Rub salt over cracked egg and you can successfully boil it.

If only half of an onion is needed, save the root half. It will last longer.

To keep bread fresh, store a celery rib in the package.

To keep noodles or rice from boiling over, add a Tbsp. of oil to the water.

Correct greasy gravy by adding a bit of baking powder.

To keep popcorn fresh and encourage more kernels to pop, store in freezer.

If soup tastes very salty, a raw piece of potato placed in the pot will absorb the salt.

1/3 c. lemon gelatin dissolved in 2 c. of hot apricot nectar with 1 tsp. of grated lemon added for zip makes a perfect base for jellied fruit salad.

If cream will not whip, add the white of an egg, or a little cornstarch.

When combining pineapple with gelatin, always scald the pineapple fruit and juice first, or the jelly will not set.

In keeping vegetables fresh, place them in a deep dish in about 2" of cold water, then take a piece of clean linen, soak it in water, and cover the vegetables, letting the corners of the cloth dip into the water to keep it moist, then place the dish on a window sill where the air will blow over it.

All grease which is not suitable for cooking purposes can be used up with lye to make soap for kitchen use.

Regulate the oven carefully before starting to mix the ingredients for baking.

To frost a cake evenly, use a double piece of stiff paper and pin it closely about the cake, letting the paper extend about an inch over the top of the cake, spread the icing and when icing has set, remove the paper.

Before adding gelatin to a hot liquid, soak gelatin in a cold liquid.

Canned fruits become richer in flavor if opened an hour before using.

Left-over fruit juice, coffee, or chocolate can be made into delicious sweet sauces.

Milk will not scorch so easily when heating in saucepan, if you rinse the pan with water first.

You should not pile together left-over potatoes, as they sour quickly.

Make a holder for your cookbook, by pushing in the sides of a wire clothes hanger, shaping it lengthwise. Next fold the lower half up shaping it so it will hold the book when open. Hang it on a knob of your cupboards. Put your cookbook in while using it. This will help keep the book clean and makes it easy to read.

In a custard recipe calling for several eggs, 1 or more may be left out if $1/2$ Tbsp. cornstarch is added for each egg omitted.

To beat the white part of an egg quickly, have it room temperature and add a pinch of salt.

Onion odor may be removed from hands by rubbing them with dry salt.

Cleaning Hints

Using liquid Ivory at your wash basin to wash your hands and face leaves such a clean basin. No build-up of standing water and soap. No messy soap dish to clean or fall on the floor. Put liquid Ivory in a dispenser with a small hole, or push the opener of bottle down a little.

Saucepans that are badly burned can be cleaned by boiling in water to which a handful of salt has been added.

An excellent way to remove soot from a carpet is to sprinkle the place thickly with salt. Sweep up the salt and the soot will come along.

To pick up broken glass use a wet paper towel, its better than sweeping it together.

To clean a grease laden oven, place 2 pt. hot water in a pan with 2 Tbsp. ammonia and let it set in your oven overnight. It should clean easily by morning.

Use hot vinegar to remove paint splashes from glass.

Put a few drops of lemon juice in a grinder before you grind sticky fruit. The grinder will be easier to clean.

Remove ballpoint pen ink stains with hair spray.

With a medicine dropper, apply glycerin as a lubricant for egg beaters, etc., having moving parts. The glycerin will not spoil the taste of the food if mixed in accidently.

Next time you boil potatoes, soak tarnished silverware in the cooking water for about an hour. Your silverware will come out looking like new.

Stains on a sink or bathtub often can be removed with a paste of hydrogen peroxide and cream of tartar.

Machine oil sometimes will help eradicate scratches on furniture. Rub with a soft cloth.

To keep gold or silver from tarnishing, keep wrapped in black tissue paper.

To make your glasses sparkle add a little laundry bluing to your dish water.

For sparkling windows and chrome, use ammonia water to clean them and rub dry with crumpled newspapers.

On Birds

Birdbaths. Here's how you coax birds into the birdbath: Put some sand on the bottom and few seeds on the surface of the water.

If it's in the sun, move it to the shade. The water may be too warm.

"Cheep" Birdseed. Dried seeds from melons, pumpkins, or squash make great birdseed.

Transfer birdseed from the original box to an empty salt carton for easy pouring.

Miscellaneous

If you need an ice bag in a hurry and don't have one, fill a rubber glove with crushed ice and tie securely at the wrist.

To prevent broken china when washing dishes place a thick folded cloth in the bottom of the pan.

The kids will love this one. Roll up a dollar bill and insert it into a balloon. Mail it along in a card with instructions to blow up and pop. Or insert an invitation to a party with the same instructions to blow up and pop.

Old Saying: Three months after the first Katydid begins "hollering", the first killing frost will come.

For rough red hands, try putting a 1/2 tsp. of sugar in the palm of your hand and soak the sugar up with mineral or baby oil. Massage hands briskly for a few minutes. Then wash with soapy water.

To remove super-glue from your hands, do not just peel off or your skin will peel off also. Soak area with nail polish remover until the glue disappears.

For sweaty feet: Wash in borax every night.

A plastic hanging plant pot makes a great weatherproof clothespin holder for the clothesline. When it rains, the water will drain out of the holes in the planter's bottom.

Use a bobby pin to hold a nail or tack in place as you hammer to avoid smashed fingers.

Calcium makes strong Teeth and Bones

Foods that are excellent sources of calcium:

Milk: whole or skimmed; dried or evaporated
Green leafy vegetables: turnip and mustard greens, kale, collards, broccoli, dandelion greens, watercress.
Cheese: Swiss, American or cheddar
Navy beans.
Molasses.

Iron Builds Red Blood

Foods that are excellent sources of iron:

Eggs.
Green leafy vegetables.
Liver, heart.
Oysters, shrimp.
Meats, lean.
Poultry, dark meat.
Whole-grain breads, cereals, enriched breads.
Molasses, sorgo syrup.
Fruits, dried: apricots, peaches, prunes, raisins.
Beans: common, kidney, lima, lentils, soybeans.
Iron in foods is measured by a weight called a milligram. (The head of a common pin weighs 1 milligram.)
1000 milligrams equal 1 gram.
1 ounce equals about 30 grams.

Body Building Proteins

Foods that are sources of protein:

Complete—Milk, cheese, eggs, lean meats, poultry, fish, peanuts, soybeans.

Index

Desserts

Meats and Vegetables

Miscellaneous

Pies

Preserving Foods

Salads, Sandwiches and Drinks

Soups